Practical Credit Scoring:
Issues and Techniques

MURRAY BAILEY

White Box Publishing

Published by

White Box Publishing
291 New Cheltenham Road
Kingswood
Bristol BS15 4RD

Trademarks
Many words in this publication that the authors and publisher believe to be trademarks, have been designated as such by use of initial capital letters. In so designating or failing to designate such words, neither the authors nor the publisher intends to express any judgment on the validity or legal status of any proprietary right that may be claimed in the words.

ISBN 0 - 9540053 - 5 - X

pancredit **systems**

Established in 1988, **pan**credit is a leading provider of lending system solutions specialising in developing, implementing and supporting loan administration systems.

pancredit's system covers the entire life-cycle of a finance agreement for medium and large organisations operating in consumer finance, motor finance, asset finance and insurance premium finance. From the initial customer enquiry and underwriting through to servicing and completion, **pan**credit supports all types of lending products including hire purchase, personal loans, revolving credit, motor finance, leasing and insurance premium finance products.

pancredit has been awarded the international security standard BS7799 (ISO 17799) complementing its seven year registration against the international quality standard ISO 9001 and its associated 'TickIT' certification. Furthermore, **pan**credit has been informally rated at Level 2/3 of the US based Capability Maturity Model.

For further information please visit www.pancredit.com

Windsor CME

Windsor CME provides independent solutions for the consumer credit industry.

Our Credit Academy training services cover marketing, collections and risk and include the two scorecard courses: "The Ten Tools of Credit Scoring" and "Advanced Credit Scoring: Issues and Techniques".

At Windsor we pride ourselves at building solutions that balance technical expertise with practicality. This is illustrated by our ClearScore scorecard development software which enables developers to involve the operation either challenging the scorecard or as a training tool.

For more information on Windsor CME's services, please email: admin@windsorcme.co.uk For details of courses and booking, visit our website: www.windsorcme.co.uk

CONTENTS

PREFACE

After many years of training people in building and tracking scorecards, I collaboratively produced "Credit Scoring: The Principles and Practicalities". In designing the original book I wanted to avoid the basics of scoring that were adequately covered elsewhere – in particular I did not want to reproduce Edward Lewis' famous introductory book. The result was a range of chapters that covered many of the advanced issues, some of which were from user perspectives. Whilst the book has sold very well, I was left unsatisfied.

One of our courses is called "Advanced Credit Scoring: Issues and Techniques". The original book didn't cover many of the challenges that developers face and I found myself contrasting some of the chapters in the original book with the experiences discussed in the course. It finally struck me that the only way I would be satisfied would be to write the book myself and include much of the material of the course. I didn't want to write a stodgy text book. My aim was to write something that was from a practical perspective and that would discuss the issues, pitfalls, solutions and tools. I wanted to write something semi-technical; for the developer or risk manager without too much mathematics. I have had to include equations, but I have limited these to ones that can be used as tools and have avoided the proofs.

"Practical Credit Scoring: Issues and Techniques" incorporates many of the elements of the advanced scoring course. To provide a greater breadth and interest, I have included some more introductory chapters and some from our tracking scorecard course

"The Ten Tools of Credit Scoring". Finally, as with the original book, I have sought to include helpful chapters on more advanced issues such as customer scoring, profit scoring and using scorecards for the Internal Ratings Based approach to capital.

I hope that I have succeeded in producing a document that you find of practical use. If as a result, developers build better and more widely accepted models, I will be satisfied that it was worth the effort.

Finally I would like to thank the following people for reviewing the draft and for their helpful comments: Andrew Asaam, Leigh Baker, Peter Constance and Mike Cutter.

Murray Bailey
Windsor Consulting
May 2006

INTRODUCTION

In the 50 years that credit scoring has been around, it has placed itself at the heart of lending institutions decision-making. Slowly at first, with a few companies testing the concept, then more rapidly as the concepts became more widely accepted. With wider acceptance came greater depth of information and improved technology. Scorecards, look like they do today because of the limited technology of the past; scorecards had to be integers and were additive so that operators could calculate the score and compare the result to a pass mark in their heads. By the start of the 1980's the US and UK were developing consumer credit bureaux that could capture lenders information and summarise it to aid future lending decisions. Account information sharing kick-started credit scoring as models became more complicated, sophisticated and predictive. Automation of credit bureau links enabled applicant information to be assessed rapidly and consistently. Gradually businesses overcame their reliance on subjective decision-making as the systematic, consistent approach was shown to out perform human judgement.

To assist the transition, the decision engines also improved. They moved from rule-based, hard coded software to highly parameterized flexible solutions that empowered the risk management teams. Strategy software developed so that decisions could be given extra dimensions. Applications could be segmented for different treatment and decisions progressed from one-dimensional accept or decline, to include line assignment, product features and risk based pricing.

Initially the credit bureau was seen as an expense to be saved and many early scorecards were designed with two stages. Application score followed by a final score. Applications failing the application score would not progress to the credit bureau thereby saving the cost of a search. The power of the bureau data combined with the ability to tailor offers to risk segments, has resulted in an about face: the credit bureau search is now often the first stage after sufficient identity information has been captured. Some organisations now reject applicants who don't meet credit bureau criteria, thus saving processing cost, or determine the second stage questions based upon the bureau outcome.

The 1990's saw the rapid spread of scoring as companies recovered from the Recession, realising that objective decision-making reduced operational risk, whilst statistical tools provided the control management needed to ensure the appropriate level of risk was being taken. Regulators also recognised that scoring provided an evaluation of the risk being taken by a lender and have now determined international rules for determining the level of capital that a bank should hold relative to the potential losses. As a result, what started as a trickle in the 1960's has become a flood today with the mortgage lenders and others joining the approach to underwriting and portfolio management what was started mainly by the mail order and store credit companies.

The greater the discrimination of risk, the lower the capital requirement and so the pressure is on to find new techniques and data to improve the models. In response, credit bureaus have deepened their data and models and the incorporation of these in lenders' scorecards is growing. Where a single bureau reference may be taken, some lenders now find benefit in taking multiple searches from multiple bureaus.

This book covers the practical issues of building good application and behavioural scorecards. Many assumptions are made during a development and it is imperative that both the developer and the organisation appreciate what approaches have been used and what the implications are. The growing importance of and reliance on scorecards, means that the models must be robust and practical. A scorecard that appears statistically to be highly discriminatory must deliver those benefits. Time and time again you will read that operational practicality and the strategic use of the model is more important than the new technology used to build the scorecard.

Peter Constance
Pancredit
May 2006

Practical Credit Scoring

"Most of the fundamental ideas of science are essentially
simple and may, as a rule, be expressed in a language
comprehensible to everyone."
Albert Einstein (1879 - 1955)

1

The Bad Science of Scoring

Myth

"There is a self-perpetuating industry based around the management of scoring. Large numbers of people are engaged in the establishment and verification of strategies that have been designed to be so complicated that they cannot be verified. It is one of the myths of risk management."

This quote was by the Group Credit Officer of a major international bank. In "Credit Scoring: principles and practicalities, we said that Economics has become a complete slave to optimisation. Whatever the problem in the world, there must be a function to describe it. Scoring has become the same.

Whilst on the surface this looks like a good idea - moving from subjective to objective, profit based decisions it is all too easy to lose practicality. In addition, complexity can obscure and leave the business dangerously exposed.

Credit scoring is full of assumptions and data manipulation. Spurious science is bad science.

In the 50 or so years of credit scoring, little except for the technology and speed of development and processing, has changed. Some companies and developers continue to guard their scorecards from the business in the name of integrity.

However, secrecy can hide a multitude of sins, including bad science. The remainder of this chapter is about the areas in which a scorecard developer may impact the science of the scorecard and hence the effectiveness of the decision.

The business question
What problem is the scorecard trying to address. The more specific one can be about who the decision is to be made about and what actions may result, will aid the sample design and definitions of Good and Bad.

Profitability is unlikely to be a reasonable outcome. This is because profitability is hard to establish especially on revolving products. Bear in mind that the customer has no control over the interest rate your funds cost you, nor your overheads.

The sample selection, outcome period and definitions are crucial to an effective solution. A scorecard project should therefore spend time evaluating the precise problem to be solved and which accounts are relevant to the decision.

Intermediates
Intermediates form part of the definition issue. Most business managers assume that the development was based on Goods and Bads. However, it is common to have a group of cases that are neither Good nor Bad. The choice of definition can leave an intermediate group.

The more extreme the definition of Good and Bad, the better the scorecard will appear. However, using written-off as a Bad definition and up-to-date as Good, will leave a large group of unclassified customers who are very important to the business.

The separation of Goods and Bads (measured by Gini say) can be increased by increasing the grey area. However, it can be that these customers are either profitable or unprofitable. The reality is that the business will continue to get these people and should consider whether they would want to do business with them again had they known how they would perform.

An unscrupulous or ignorant developer can therefore increase the apparent power of the scorecard at the detriment of the business.

Human error
Developers make mistakes. The most important part of scorecard development is sampling and data manipulation. The best scorecards are based on well understood data warehouses. The incorrect interpretation of a field can be dramatic. I know of one major firm who delivered a scorecard where a variable that comprised of a random number was assigned points. Criminally, the developer only realised at the last minute and disguised the variable as a valid characteristic.

Grouping
Most scorecards are developed by combining attributes (the different outcomes) of variables. This is necessary to increase cell counts of Goods and Bads and hence the statistical significance. Whilst it is possible to use continuous data, the traditional point score approach requires that variables are grouped.

A starting point may be to use time at address and ignore months, relying only on years at address. This may then be compressed down to between say two and ten attribute groups.

Time based characteristics are logical to combine, but others, such as postcode have a multitude of outcomes many of which may have too few counts to provide a reasonable reflection of the risk of a new applicant. Common sense must be used in this situation. Software that automatically groups attributes will do so using statistics based on Bad rate (such as the t-test). No common-sense is applied.

A developer can therefore produce what looks like a powerful characteristic by inappropriate combinations. I have witnessed this with a geo-demographic code which appeared predictive in the scorecard, but simply provided no discrimination in practice. (If one was cynical one could suggest that this was a deliberate to justify the purchase of the code from the credit bureau).

Missing information
Blanks appear in datasets. 'No answer' to an application form question may be a legitimate outcome. The developer needs to ask whether it is possible and can be considered - whether the attribute should be ignored or whether the record should be excluded from the sample. The developer should also question whether it occurs randomly or for a reason.

Let's consider income as a characteristic. Say that the analysis shows that it is a very powerful predictor. However, 10% of records have no income provided and these contribute greatest to the discrimination. If the business no longer allows customers to be approved without providing income details, a scorecard with this characteristic will be weaker than predicted.

Whether these records should be excluded will depend on the scenario. It could be that these are a type of customer that will not be considered in future. Imagine they are all students and the business will no longer accept students. In this case the 'no income' cases should be dropped from the sample.

Otherwise, the characteristic should be evaluated excluding the 'no income' cases. If the characteristic is considered in the regression (or other modelling technique), the 'no income' cases should usually get the no information/default points. A common practice is 'mean substitution', replacing the blank with the average for the characteristic. This can result it misleading characteristic analysis when tracking and should be used only with caution.

Sampling

The sample should be representative of the new population that the scorecard is to be applied to. The sample window should typically be at least a year so that any seasonality is taken into account. Applications should not be too old: otherwise they may not be reflective of the future applications (forms change, credit bureau data deepens, economic conditions as well as general shifts in socio-economics change).

On the other hand if applications are too recent, accounts that will become Bad are still Good. There needs to be an adequate outcome period for performance to mature. Ideally the sample (Goods, Bads and Rejects) should all be selected from the same time window.

The present is like the past

Modelling is predicated on the assumption that the future will be like the past. However, there is a dichotomy between the sample relevance and the outcome period you choose.

It may seem reasonable for a sample of closed end loans to be over the whole life. In this way Bad can be simply defined as write-off. Scorecards built this way can achieve very high Ginis. However, when implemented the performance is considerably worse than predicted. Why? Because things change. The longer you wait, the less your present is like the past.

Reject inference

If a scorecard is developed without considering past rejects, the variables that lead to the previous decision will be understated. Consider the extreme example where most applicants with adverse credit are rejected. The few that are accepted have special terms and on average perform better than the rest of the portfolio.

A scorecard developed ignoring the rejects could determine that adverse credit is in fact a good thing! As a previous applicant looks less and less like a previous accepted customer, their profile is worse and their risk of being Bad higher. The only way of proving what their performance would be is to accept them. No modelling technique is accurate and reject inference is more of an art than a science.

Overrides

Lenders who use underwriters have overrides: applicants who failed the cut-off but were accepted (usually called Lowsides) and applicants who passed but were declined (usually called Highsides). Policy declines are an example of Highsides.

Highside overrides look like the accepts, but have a characteristic that is usually not available to the developer. For example, an underwriter may have found that the employment could not be verified. In the ideal world it would be nice to have a code that reflected the exact reason for the override. However, anyone who has ever tried this finds that the majority get classed as 'other' or get a default code.

If the developer ignores the fact that the application was a Highside he will determine that the rejected application looks like an accept and could infer that the reject would have performed like a similar accept. This is highly unlikely and will have the effect of, not only inflating the Gini, but overstating the predicted acceptance rate.

If the proportion of Highsides is low the developer should probably exclude them from the sample. Some developers assign –99 points for what is effectively a policy decline.

Smoothing, rounding

The final scorecard statistics are likely to have been manipulated. The simplest example of this is the presentation of the scorecard as integers. Scorecards were designed as simply as possible because they had to be easy to add up mentally. Today this is no longer a factor, but we still prefer integers because it looks neater.

Where small samples are used, the statistics can show anything but smooth distributions. This doesn't look nice and some developers will smooth the distribution out, arguing that the distortions are due to the statistical fluctuations that will not be reflected in practice. The effect of smoothing can be in to increase the Gini and may hide an aberration in the scorecard.

Factoring

Most scorecards are developed on samples that require factoring up to reflect the true population. For example, traditionally 1,500 Goods, Bads and Rejects are used and the final distributions changed to reflect the true proportions.

However, the Gini, which depends on the contribution of the different groups (Goods, Bads, inferred Goods and inferred Bads), will change. The Gini for the final population will be higher than the development sample. The biggest impact is the factor applied to the Rejects.

Conclusions

Scorecard development has become quite a science. However, much of the modelling and manipulation has been judgmental. The solution is therefore to involve the business in the design and development to ensure practicality and understanding.

Something that scorecard developers and risk managers must appreciate that the goal is not to produce the highest Gini. The true value of a scorecard is to deliver real benefits and improvements to the business.

In later chapters we will look at the detail of many of the issues discussed in this chapter. One of the main principles to guide you in the review of a scorecard development, is the more understandable the model, the better it is likely to perform. As Einstein famously said, "Everything should be made as simple as possible, but not one bit simpler."

2

Building Scorecards

How it all began

Most consumer credit risk people today take credit scoring for granted. It seems obvious that we should use models to assess creditworthiness and yet it was not that long ago that more widespread acceptance was achieved. Scorecards did not explode on to the scene they stuttered into life. In the 1940's two Chicago-based companies: Household Finance and Speigal Mail Order were the first to try modelling credit losses following a research paper on the subject. Neither company succeeded; in fact it took Household 40 years to revisit the technique.

The initial problem was both complexity and acceptance. In an industry that was manually intensive, the scorecard was first thought of as a tool to help the underwriter or clerk, since computers and calculators were things of the future. Early scorecards had to be paper based and simple.

Since they were manually applied, for ease scorecards were designed with point scores that were integers and added together to give a total score. Conditional probabilities are usually multiplied together to give the total likelihood. In the late 1950's two mathematicians Bill Fair and Earl Isaac used natural logarithms to convert odds in to raw point scores (Weights of

Evidence). In this way they developed the first successful models for the American Investment Corporation (AIC) of Illinois.

The scorecard build process

We'll look at Weights of Evidence in chapter 4. Rather than use a technique such as multiple regression, Fair Isaac's original technique was to take the Weights of Evidence and iteratively step them to remove the correlation. 50 years on, some developers still prefer this approach arguing that development is more about the process than the technique used.

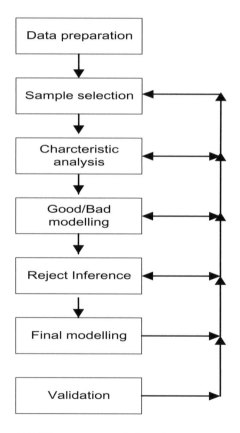

Figure 2.1 The scorecard development process

The standard modelling process dates back to the original scorecard developments. This process is shown in figure 2.1. The start is to pull the data that seems appropriate and then reduce this to a sample that is considered reliable and representative for the business need.

Figure 2.2 illustrates the sample window where applications may be selected over a 12 month period to allow for seasonality. In this example, the performance period will be an average for the applications. An alternative is to select a fixed performance period and look at the outcome for each month's business at a difference observation date.

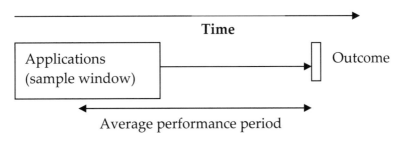

Figure 2.2 Sample window and performance period

Contingent upon this is the determination of the Good and Bad definitions. Also, we should have evaluated the appropriateness of the performance period. We will look at both of these issues in chapter 6. One tip is to look at the vintage analysis to see how the arrears has matured over time for each tranche of new business. To aid with the determination of the sample window, I recommend reviewing a table of applications by month. Calculate bad rates and override rates for each of these months to identify any unusual months or patterns. The principle we will consider when looking for enough Bads will be that data too old will not be reflective of the current business and applications too recent will not have mature enough performance to be robust enough for modelling purposes.

The Characteristic analysis stage about identifying the most reliable variables. Automated techniques can be used today to clean data, but manually reviewing the raw data counts and Characteristic Analysis is by far and away the best way to get to understand the data. Comparing the actual data with the data dictionary will highlight discrepancies and spurious codes. It will also help in the next stage which is grouping the attributes to form a statistically robust and manageable number of attributes.

The modelling stage is to build a Known Good:Bad (KGB) model. The most common technique today is stepwise logistic regression. The advice is to use one that you understand and consider the reliability based on the sample size. In chapter 8 we will consider the alternative techniques and recommend alternatives based on the sample.

Reject Inference is the process of inferring the performance of the rejected applications. The higher the proportion of rejects in the sample, the more important this will be. We need to include a prediction of the reject's performance since the improvement in a scorecard will be derived by swapping Bad accepts for Good rejects. We will see in chapter 9 that we need to consider the reject distribution to appropriately assign a predicted risk to a rejected application. Characteristic Analysis of the rejects may prompt reconsideration of the attribute groups. This illustrates a point: a good developer will be prepared to go back to any stage of the development and, based on results, redo an earlier stage.

The final modelling stage is then to build a model using both the accepts and the rejects. The final set of statistics will be produced from this scorecard. The distributions are usually referred to as 'run books'. It is best practice to produce these for the weighted and unweighted sample and provide performance of all categories so that a user can plot the score-odds of the rejects and any sub-groups such as overrides or Not Taken Ups (NTUs) – the applications that were accepted but didn't become loans.

Figure 2.3 shows a population flow which illustrates the outcome classification and reject inference. Where there has been sampling, it should also inform the user of the sample ratios. This provides the opportunity to ensure that the appropriate factors are re-applied to the figures before attempting to align a scorecard or calculate cut-off strategies. Note that where NTUs occur significantly, the developer will need to consider how to handle these and should include them in the population flow.

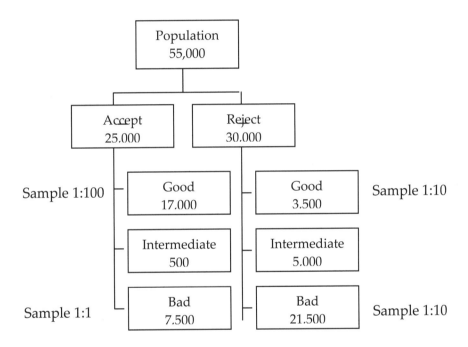

Figure 2.3 Final population flow

Validation will often start with comparing the results with a Hold-out sample. A developer should look at the difference in Gini, for example and the improvement in decisions resulting from a selected cut-off. Other validation approaches include comparison with a recent sample and we shall look at all of these in chapter 10.

Project management

Overlying the flow chart in figure 2.1 must be the principles of good project management. In fact some would begin the chart with 'project management' to emphasise its importance.

One bank commissioned external scorecard developers to rebuild its three scorecards. The existing scorecards were unsecured personal loans split by financed product: Electrical goods, Motor vehicles and Home Improvements. The developer did an immaculate job and delivered three new scorecards that reduced risk by almost 10%. They had built scorecards split by age group: under 26, 26 to 34 and over 35. Each scorecard showed strong separation of the Goods and Bads, however they could not be implemented.

There had been good communication between the developer and the scorecard analysts at the bank. However, the only communication with the application processing unit came when the scorecards were presented for approval prior to implementation. There were two issues that the operation immediately recognised:
- the structure of the operation, and
- the impact on each product.

Each of the three products had a different system. It made sense for the systems to be integrated but that project was many years away. This meant that the scorecards could not be physically implemented without significant screen and process flow redesign. Secondly, the benefits were not evenly distributed throughout the products. The main benefit was for Electrical. Motor reduced acceptance and Home Improvements was unchanged. This was an issue, because, not only was Motor unable to reduce acceptance rates due to dealer pressure, it was also more profitable than Electrical.

So communication with the business at an early stage is vital to a successful implementation. A plan must start with a clearly defined objective, one that is business oriented. The objective of improving the separation of goods and bads is not well defined enough. This stage may help in the choice of outcome definitions as well as identify problem or necessary characteristics. The plan should also include:

- What is to be done and how
- A work breakdown
- Key milestones
- Responsibilities
- Project control

Conclusion

There is a best practice approach to scorecard development. The worst developments are ones which do not follow the rigor of this process. Planning, communication and documentation are watchwords for any project and certainly apply to scorecard development. There are many areas in which mistakes can be made and a bad scorecard may not just deliver sub-optimal results they can even damage a business.

3

Underwriting and Scoring

Underwriting

Underwriting is the assessment and verification of three elements:

- Capacity to pay
- Character
- Collateral

The extent of credit investigation depends on the exposure to credit loss. This depends on the amount lent and product and will typically have a relationship indicated in figure 3.1. The greater the money at risk, the greater the justification of manually intensive underwriting. A mortgage will therefore justify a significant amount of investigation into the applicant's ability to repay and the value of the property whereas a store card or mail order account is most likely to be approaching 100 percent automation.

Pre-screening and Superfails

There is no point in incurring processing costs for applications that have no hope of approval. Lenders therefore advertise their minimum criteria to discourage such applications. These may be based on:

- Minimum age

- Minimum income
- Forms of identity
- Employment criteria
- Country of residence
- Arrears or bankruptcy history

For mortgages there is usually a 'mortgage calculator' that acts as a screen to enable the prospective applicant calculate whether their desired loan amount is realistic based on their income.

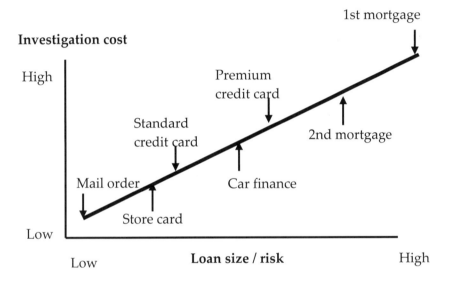

Figure 3.1: Investigation cost by credit product

Again, to keep processing costs to a minimum, certain 'no hoper' applications will be immediately rejected by the system. These cases are often called *Superfails* because they are out-and-out rejects. Examples of these are likely to include the criteria listed in the pre-screen rules. In addition there may be automatic declines based on:

- Credit score
- Bureau reference
- Fraud
- Affordability

- Loan to value for mortgages

Where the credit reference occurs after an initial application score, Superfails refers to applications that are rejected prior to requesting a credit reference. This approach is to save on credit bureau costs although this practice is less common in countries where the credit bureaux are advanced and make up the majority of the discrimination by the decision system.

Applications may also be automatically rejected if mandatory fields are not completed. However, most companies will have a process for returning applications requesting the additional information.

Judgement vs. credit scoring

Credit scoring enables a lender to rapidly assess the credit worthiness of an applicant. For the lower value risk products head to head tests of scoring vs. human judgement has shown scoring to out perform traditional underwriting. The advantage of credit scoring is that it can be automated, thus delivering a rapid, low cost decision to the applicant. The issues with human judgement are: inconsistency, lack of management control, lack of quantification of risk and motivation

Even when underwriters are operating within guidelines, being consistent is impossible. Decisions can vary from day to day and particularly where there is direct contact with the underwriter (especially brokers or other intermediaries) there can be tremendous pressure on the underwriter to make 'one-off' exceptions. The underwriter may be called upon to make character assessments even though the information is second hand.

Credit scoring provides a sliding scale with which to adjust the quality accepted by the business. Underwriters cannot provide this level of fine tuning. There is no tap to slightly turn. With underwriters it tends to be an 'on/off' switch. There is also a lack of flexibility with underwriting (or policy) rules. These rules tend to be fixed, such as 'no arrears'. Whereas scoring considers this in conjunction with the other information and can determine the appropriate weight to this information.

Scoring also provides statistics against which the business can be measured and tracked. This quantification provides a benchmark that underwriting can only be, and indeed should be measured against.

Finally, there is always the risk of a conflict of objectives. Where underwriting is part of a branch operation or a central function that reports to a head with short term profit objectives, the pressure may be to achieve volume and approval rates at the expense of quality. Without scoring, the business may not appreciate that the pressure to improve customer service (through higher acceptance rates) is resulting in a decline in quality. Feedback of performance of the underwriting decisions is therefore vital in establishing control over quality. Where commission is paid based on sales, the conflict can be solved by relating the payout of the commission or bonuses to the achievement of quality targets.

Case study
The interaction of underwriters with scoring can be a complicated one. This is especially the case for motor finance where applications may be re-proposed to find terms that are acceptable to the lender. The problem with this is that the terms of the deal are often in the scorecard.

Motor finance scorecards often have vehicle details in them as well as deal terms such as instalment, loan term and loan to value. Deposit is often a powerful predictor. It indicates the investment in the vehicle by the purchaser. However, lenders rarely know whether the deposit is cash, funded by another loan or a trade in. In other words, there are degrees of reliability.

Auto Finance (as we'll call them) was typical of motor finance companies. Loans were secured on the vehicle (Hire Purchase) and decisioned using both scorecards and underwriters. Underwriters reviewed every application. Applications passing the cut-off, were not automatically accepted. The price of the vehicle was checked against the trade price and details of income and expenditure were checked against an affordability matrix. The underwriters also acted as a fraud detection team, looking for unusual details or keeping an eye on specific areas or salesmen.

Applications failing the cut-off were not automatically rejected. Underwriters would discuss a score-failure with the dealership and look for opportunity to approve the case. 'Working the deal' consisted of adjusting the deal details to achieve a score-pass since applications were not approved below the cut-off. The applications processed by Auto Finance had no audit trail. A test on a small sample showed that, on average, an application would be scored at least twice as underwriters tried different terms to increase the score.

Figure 3.2 shows the score distribution. The 'Observed' applications are the final scores and there are clearly two bulges in the distribution. The peak occurring at 80 to 89 points was caused by a sub-population of older applicants. The area of interest is just above the cut-off of 40. Based on final scores, 8.1% were expected to fail the cut-off, but only 6.8% actually did. Instead of average score of 63, the average was 58, reflecting the lower than expected profile of applications and approved loans. The underwriters were not only using their knowledge of the scorecard to increase acceptance, but they were also working with the dealerships to enable more favourable terms to be offered, such as larger loans and lower deposits.

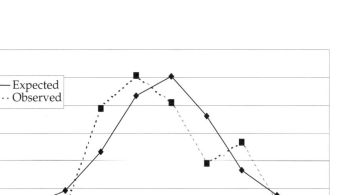

Figure 3.2: Actual vs. Expected application distributions

Figure 3.3 is the analysis of deposit. This chart shows that 15 to 24 percent was a higher risk indicator than would be expected. Typically risk decreases as deposit size increases. Further analysis identified that the problem deposit was exactly 15 percent - the point at which applicants scored significantly more.

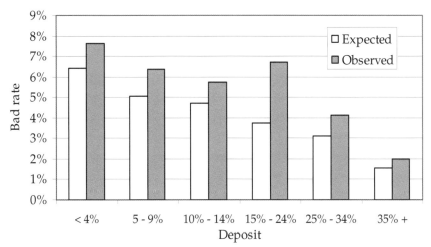

Figure 3.3: Bad rates by deposit

The Underwriter Effect

Underwriters therefore create a problem for the scorecard developer. Traditionally, scorecard developers are careful about the security of the scorecard characteristics and weights since scorecards can be undermined by the manipulation of data.

However, from the Underwriters' perspective, the motor and finance details are not fixed when a customer walks through the door. Many vehicles are sold based on their monthly instalment, rather than their price. Affordability is often the primary consideration. Secondary to this are the deposit and loan term. Without knowledge of the vehicle and finance elements of the scorecard, the salesman makes his 'best guess' at the finance company's requirements.

In an attempt to support the salesmen, the underwriters will usually have a good understanding of the scorecard. It is not uncommon for Underwriters to test scorecards by trying different combinations of detail. Over a short period of time they can become quite proficient at knowing what is required to turn a score-fail into an acceptable application.

There is no simple solution to using scorecards where predictive information can be adjusted. The key for the business is to monitor the underwriters' performance. Analysis by risk grade or score band will enable a fairer comparison of the risk and acceptance rate relationship. In fact a useful ratio is:

Decision ratio = Acceptance rate / Bad rate

The higher the decision ratio, for a given score band, the better the decisions.

Conclusion

A scorecard developer should always look at whether there is a strong influence by the underwriters and compare this with the objective of the business. If the objective is to automate more, then the scorecard should try to reflect the underwriter's experience. Otherwise the scorecard should be there to support the underwriting activity.

Remember that scoring looks at risk from a stability aspect rather than ability to pay today. Bad was defined in a specific manner to build a robust scorecard and yet this definition includes a whole range of subsets of high risk customer: some of whom couldn't pay after a period of time, some couldn't pay at the out set and some have a poor attitude to credit. It tries to combine each of the three elements of underwriting and in so doing is an approximation of each. Underwriters may be better placed to assess affordability and evidence of portfolios getting this wrong is where there is a high proportion of early defaulters.

4

The Value of Data

The Principles and sources

There are two principles about the use of data for scorecard development. Firstly, the better the data, the better the resultant model. Secondly, if it is legally available, evaluate it for use in the scorecard.

There are three types of data that should be considered for inclusion in application scorecard development:

- application form data
- credit reference information
- existing account information

Application data is taken at the time of application and should include both accepted and rejected applications. Rejects are necessary to fairly represent the complete 'through-the-door' population, since it is to this group that the scorecard will be applied.

Any additional information disclosed or uncovered following investigation by underwriters should also be included. If the underwriters discover application information is inaccurate, both pieces of information are relevant. Wherever possible, avoid overwriting details; errors and falsification can be just as predictive and sometimes more illuminating than accurate information.

The second category of data is all the bureau information at the time of the application or decision. This is ideally captured at the point of application. However, credit reference agencies typically provide a service whereby data is recreated retrospectively.

The existing account data arises where a previous relationship has existed and contains performance information more detailed than that held by the credit reference agency. Own account information may be available real-time, whereas bureau data can be up to two months old.

Characteristics are either continuous or discrete (categorical). Examples of continuous variables are: age, time at address and credit turnover. Examples of discrete variables are: residential status, marital status and worst arrears status.

A key driver of characteristic interpretation is the number of accounts that can be analysed. In most application scorecard developments, the number of bad accounts is limited and this becomes the main determinant for banding or grouping the attributes. The first stage for continuous variables is often to band them into manageable groups, for example converting time at address to years at address.

Characteristic power

Chi-Squared and the Gini coefficient may be used to identify the strength of characteristics, however Information Value can provide the developer with greater insight since it relates directly to the Weights of Evidence.

Information odds are the ratio of goods to bads where the overall population risk has been removed by comparing equal numbers or percentages of the goods and bads. In the equation below,

%Good$_a$ is the percentage of the goods with attribute 'a' and %Bad$_a$ is the percentage of the bads with attribute 'a'.

$$WoE_a = Ln(\%Good_a/\%Bad_a)$$

Since WoE$_a$ reflects the discrimination for attribute 'a' of a characteristic, combining all WoEs provides a measure of the power of the whole characteristic. This is the Information Value. Information Value measures the separation of the goods and bads by the characteristic, assuming it to be the only variable in the scorecard.

$$\text{Information Value}_c = \Sigma\ (\%Good_a - \%Bad_a) \times WoE_a$$

Table 4.1 is an example of an Information Value calculation where the Information Value is the sum of the WoE for each attribute after it is weighted by the difference in proportions of goods and bads.

Attribute	Information Odds	Weight of Evidence	%Good - %Bad	I.V. contribution
< 25	0.571	-0.560	-15%	0.084
25 - 34	1.000	0.000	0%	0.000
35 +	1.428	0.357	15%	0.054
		Information Value:		**0.138**

Table 4.1 Example Information Value table

There are no statistical tables or significant tests for Information Value, however the interpretation is provided in table 4.2. For our Age of applicant example the Information Value is 0.138 which is an average strength for a scorecard characteristic.

Information Value	Interpretation
Less than 0.03	Poor predictor
0.03 to 0.09	Weak characteristic
0.10 to 0.29	Average characteristic
0.30 to 0.49	Strong characteristic
Over 0.50	Very strong characteristic

Table 4.2 Interpretation guide for Information Value

Trade-off between acceptance and risk

Whilst Information Value provides a statistical test of significance, it does not reflect the impact of the scorecard on the business decision; the trade off between acceptance rate and the bad rate.

Figure 4.1 is a trade-off chart for a scorecard used for credit card applications. As the acceptance rate increases, so does the bad rate. Hence, the scorecard is discriminating and the degree of discrimination is reflected by the gradient of the curve.

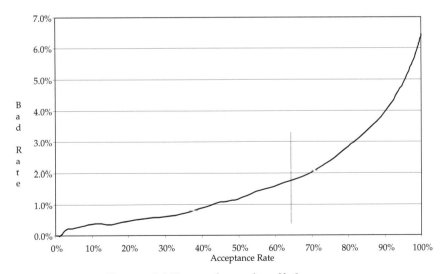

Figure 4.1 Example trade-off chart

If the business has a cut-off that delivers an acceptance rate of 66%, the bad rate is predicted to be 1.9%. This same chart can be used for assessing the impact and contribution of characteristics.

The most common form of scorecard development today is 'step-wise' regression. Characteristics are stepped into the model one at a time to avoid inclusion of unnecessary or weak variables. Characteristics can also be 'stepped out' of the development, thereby providing a result that can directly reflect the contribution of the characteristic. For example, at the same acceptance rate we could compare the bad rate before and after removal.

If the 'stepping out' process is used during development, the other point scores will change to compensate for correlation. However, simple removal without redevelopment can also provide a quick guide to the maximum impact of missing characteristics.

Case study
For the purposes of confidentiality, I shall not use the real names of the banks concerned. When two banks merged - West and North Bank - no one realised the implications for the decision systems would be so great. Both banks had well-established scoring systems, however the similarity ended there. The systems and platforms for the systems were disparate. In addition, West Bank had developed complex models that relied more on bureau data and current account performance than application information.

West Bank had developed a complex bespoke credit reference link. This unique link allowed West Bank to create their own bureau characteristics rather than rely on those generated by the bureau. North Bank had a standard link with a different bureau.

After two years of running in parallel, the inevitable decision was made to have a single, enterprise system. The West Bank team assumed it would be their more advanced solution that would survive.

The decision went the other way. The North Bank platform was newer and more widely in operation, so the application scoring system and bureau link would be theirs.

In response, the West Bank team proposed the enhancement of the newer system to meet their needs. This was rejected. The systems team were involved in the 'Year 2000' changes and there was no internal resource. Due to the same issue, all external development had been frozen. The West Bank team was instructed to redevelop their scorecards, based on the information available to North's system.

The data gap
Since good scorecard development is time consuming, whilst they began the redevelopment, the West Bank team calculated the impact of the missing data. They looked at the change in acceptance rate for the same bad rate and the change in bad rate for the same acceptance rate. This was called the 'data gap'.

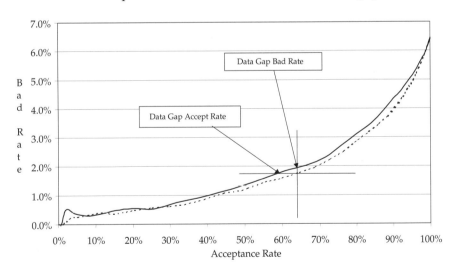

Figure 4.2 Trade off charts for credit cards

West Bank had three main portfolios: credit cards, personal loans and overdrafts. The trade-off charts for the three main scorecards are shown in figures 4.2 to 4.4. The dotted line is the original trade-off chart. The solid line is the trade-off chart assuming the loss of characteristics using North's system – without redevelopment.

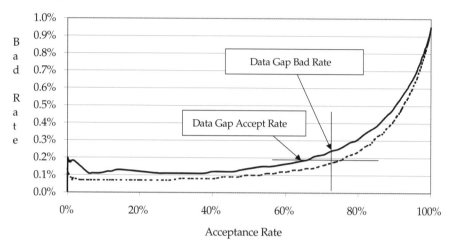

Figure 4.3 Trade off charts for personal loan

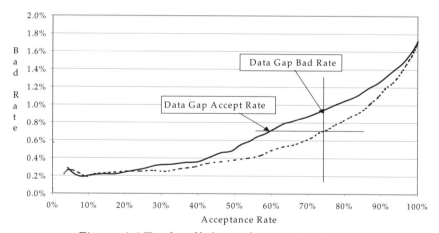

Figure 4.4 Trade off charts for overdrafts

For the credit card, personal loan and overdraft portfolios, the acceptance rates were: 66%, 75% and 74% respectively. The data gap in acceptance rates (at the same bad rates) were 5%, 15% and 10% respectively. The data gaps in bad rates (at the same acceptance rate) were 0.13%, 0.24% and 0.07% respectively.

The average deterioration in bad rate due to loss of the characteristics was 10% (an average data gap of 0.14%). The biggest impact was clearly on the personal loan. The greater impact on the personal loan new business is clearly seen in figure 4.3, which shows a greater separation of the two lines. This was to be expected due to the high level of cross-sell of the personal loan to existing customers. The credit card scorecard was least impacted because the population was more generic with a high proportion of applicants new to the bank.

Loss impact

The Credit Manager presented the charts to the management committee and pointed out the impact on write-offs. If the acceptance rates were maintained, the loss of the characteristics would mean an additional write-off per year of approximately £2.7 million.

Product	New Business	Average Write-off	Bad rate	Bad rate data gap	Write-off Impact
Credit cards	500,000	£2,300	1.70%	0.13%	£1.50m
Personal loans	200,000	£2,600	0.74%	0.24%	£1.15m
Overdrafts	300,000	£1,000	0.18%	0.07%	£0.21m
Total	900,000	£2,066	1.04%	0.15%	£2.66m

Table 4.3 Annual credit loss impact by product

The Credit Manager also pointed out that the manner in which West Bank had created the characteristics. The unique variables provided a competitive advantage that was demonstrated by the impact on losses but also customer value and cross-sell opportunity.

The priority associated with the scorecards suddenly changed. Clearly the Year 2000 system enhancements took priority, but after that came the enhancement of North's system to handle the bureau link and new scoring characteristics. The West Bank team also completed the redevelopment of the scorecards with and without the jeopardised characteristics. The revised scorecards, including the unique characteristics, achieved improvements over and above those shown in figures 4.2 to 4.4.

Conclusion

The power of a scorecard comes from the quality of the data. For characteristics to be predictive, that data must be as accurate and complete as possible. The case study demonstrated that restricting critical data can have a large financial impact on the business: poor discrimination means a poorer trade-off and the result will be higher credit losses for the same acceptance rate.

5

The Good, the Bad and the Ugly

What is Bad?

Fundamentally we would want to define Bad as a customer with whom we would not have done business had we known about his performance in advance.

Ideally we would classify the write-offs as the Bads, but it often (hopefully) takes too long to wait for all the write-offs. If a developer classifies all write-offs over the life of a portfolio as Bad and all non-write-offs as Good, the Gini of the resulting scorecard is usually very high. The problem is that the oldest write-off might be so old that the characteristics that were predictive when it was booked are less reflective of the current business. There is also an issue of whether the business will be happy to approve customers who spend time in collections but do not progress to write-off. There may also be a problem with timing of the write-off if different term loans are available in a portfolio. The result will be a variable performance period.

Figure 5.1 illustrates the ideal single Performance period where the proportion ever bad flattens. Sometimes this doesn't occur over a reasonable time frame and the developer is forced to select a shorter period. It is good practice to check the proportion becoming Bad over this period to ensure it is in excess of 50% of the accounts that are ever Bad.

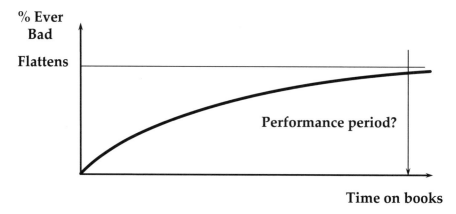

Figure 5.1 Selecting a Performance period

The definition of Bad and Performance period are dependent on one another. They are therefore often found by a process of iteration. Whilst regulators may look for 12 month outcomes for capital adequacy purposes, personal loan scorecards may have 18 month Performance periods whereas credit cards are more likely to be nearer 24 months, for example.

The solution to the Bad definition problem is therefore to find a proxy for write-off. The proxy must be reliable, stable, measurable and provide sufficient data. Bad is usually defined as a level of arrears; either current arrears or maximum (historical) arrears. The latter provides more Bads, whereas, it can be argued that the current arrears definition more fairly reflects the probability of write-off.

There are three ways Bad is often set:
- Historical precedence
- Management or consultant preferences
- Statistically.

The statistical approach is to use roll rates. Ideally these will be over the Performance period, but an annual probability of write-off will be better than nothing if the full analysis is not available.

Roll rates

Table 5.1 illustrates a range of potential Bad definitions for a scorecard development. The '% Write-off' column is the percentage of the cases that were in the category at the observation point that were written off 12 months later.

Definition	% Write-off
Currently 1 down	12%
Ever 1 down	8%
Currently2 down	33%
Ever 2 down	18%
Currently 3 down	56%
Ever 3 down	52%
Ever 2 x 2 down	20%
Ever 3 x 2 down	54%
Currently 2 down and ever 3+	54%
Currently 2 down and 3 x 1down	50%

Table 5.1 Roll rate analysis example

From this we see a number of potential Bad definitions such as 'currently 3 down' or 'ever 3 x 2 down' for example.

We could stop there, however the alternatives suggest that a combination of definitions might be appropriate. If we look at the definitions with over 50% and both rank them and make them hierarchical so that later definitions exclude accounts included in earlier ones we get the results in table 5.2.

Now we see that the 'currently 3 down' definition includes most of the cases that are picked up by the other definitions. However we can extend the definition of Bad to be 'currently 3 down or currently 2 down and ever 3'.

Definition	% Write-off
Currently 3 down	56%
Currently 2 down and ever 3	50%
Currently 2 down and 3 x 1 down	47%
Ever 3 down	31%
Ever 2 down	18%

Table 5.2 Hierarchical definition example

The practicality of the definition is not important. The business may track a totally different measure as a key quality metric. This doesn't matter. What does matter is that the bad rate the developer defines should be trackable. Scorecard performance – quite distinct from portfolio monitoring – should be based on the bad definition used to build the scorecard.

Intermediates

Intermediates are the 'grey' cases: the performance that is defined as neither Good nor Bad. Some developers define Intermediates and others refuse to have them. The larger the proportion of Intermediates the more distinct the definitions of Good and Bad will be. The more distinct the performance definition, the higher the better the discrimination between Goods and Bads will be.

However, a higher Gini does not necessarily mean a better scorecard. This is because the business will have Intermediates and will not have assessed these in trade-off considerations.

The advice is that if the business and developer are convinced that there should be an Intermediate category, then their impact should be immaterial. Keep Intermediates to less than 5% of the sample. In assessing the performance of the scorecard, the Intermediates should be added back in to the population. Look at the score distribution: where do the Intermediates lie. They will impact the acceptance rates so the 'run books' should be produced including the missing applications.

Exclusions

Not all applications will be considered in the development of a scorecard. Applications dropped are known as 'exclusions'. The developer is trying to build a model to reflect a business decision. Certain cases will be inappropriate for inclusion for this assessment. Staff or VIPs are common examples.

A scorecard developed for assessment of 'premier' customers should not include 'standard' applications. If students do not get assessed by the scorecard, they should be excluded from the sample.

Other exclusions may be ones declined for policy reasons. For example if applicants with adverse credit are policy declined and will continue to be declined, then they should be excluded.

Fraudulent applicants are a category that often gets grouped with the Bads. However, the predictive attributes of frauds are different to other Bads and due to manipulation of application details the frauds can often look like Goods. It is best practice to identify and exclude frauds and develop a separate detection program for these applications. 'Straight through bads', in other words, accounts that have never paid are usually classed with the frauds whether confirmed or not.

Store cards suffer from a phenomenon known as 'hit and run'. This is where an applicant accepts the credit to obtain a discount, settles the account in full and never uses the facility again. IKANO Financial Services in the UK always excludes the 'hit and runs' from developments. They argue that identifying these customers as Good would encourage approval of such cases. Classifying them as Bad would undermine the scorecard since they look like the Goods. This works since IKANO track Bad rates that exclude the inactives. After the development they produce the 'run books' including and excluding the 'hit and runs' so that they understand the expected acceptance rates during discount and non-discount periods.

Conclusion

The determination of the definitions of Good and Bad and which cases should be included in the development is critical to the success of the scorecard. The starting point should always be: what are we trying to achieve and which customers represent the cases we want to distinguish between?

If in doubt, look at the score distribution of excluded categories and ask whether the scorecard decisions will be appropriate for the business objective.

The developer should document the choices and note the proportions in the original population and the final modelled sample. It is best practice to reproduce the final statistics including Intermediates and exclusions that reflect the population the operation will see through-the-door. This will enable the business to make decisions that correspond to reality rather than the sample modelled.

6

Does Size Matter?

How big a sample?
Ask any developer and the usual answer is that you need 1,500
Goods, 1,500 Bads and 1,500 Rejects. This sample size paradigm
dates back to the first Fair Isaac scorecards and was their
standard. Remember this was a time when computers were in
their infancy and most of the data capture was manual.

Some developers will build models on very few Bads and
company's may have a policy of a minimum number of Bads for
their models. Indeed, the lowest I've come across is 200 Bads for a
'Basel PD model'. The problem is that these rules tend to be
judgemental rather than statistically based.

A statistical rule of thumb for modelling is that there should be at
least 50 cases in the sample for each possible outcome. If we have
a scorecard with 15 characteristics (m) of which has 5 attributes (n)
we need at least 2,800 in our sample (i.e. 14 x 4 x 50).

$$\text{Sample} > (m - 1) \times (n - 1) \times 50$$

This also serves to illustrate the point that it is not the number of
Bads that matter, but the sample size – and as we'll see later – the
bad rate.

Statistics

The truth is, the sample you require depends on the outcome you expect and the improvement you want to see.

The more we test, the closer we get to the answer. It also follows that the larger the sample, the more reliable the result. The more accurate we want to be – so that a smaller difference is significant, the larger the sample needs to be. We tend to understand this in response rate terms and are used to quoting 95% confidence levels, but we need to think about accuracy for scorecard bad rates as well.

For example, if we expect a response rate of 3% and we are looking for an improvement of 0.2% (let's assume we are therefore going to say that a result of 3.2% or better is significant at the 95% confidence level) then we will need to mail at least 29,000 letters.

The sample size is calculated by using the binomial approximation of the Normal distribution. If the result is binomial, for example a single response rate R%, we can estimate the standard deviation and z becomes $\sqrt{(R \times (100 - R))}/\sqrt{n}$. Our error at the 95% confidence level (where z is approximately 2) is:

$$\text{Error (E)} = 2\sqrt{(R \times (100 - R))}/\sqrt{n}$$

We can therefore turn this equation around to determine what my sample size should be. For an error of E, we must have a sample of at least:

$$\text{Sample size} > R \times (100 - R) \times (2/E)^2$$

When you are determining your sample size you therefore need to decide:

- How confident do I need to be (usually 95%)?
- What improvement do I want to see?
- How long do I want to wait? (the Performance period)

Scorecard errors

Now let's apply this to an application scorecard. If our bad rate is 3% and our sample size is 4,500, then the error is approximately 0.5% (i.e. 2 x √(3 x 97) / √4500).

If we have 10 equal score bands each with 450 accounts and in the top score band the bad rate is 0.3%, then the error is 0.5% (i.e. 2 x √(.3 x 99.7) / √450). This means that at the 95% confidence level our predicted bad rate for the top score band is between 0 and 0.8%.

Figure 6.1 illustrates the overall error in bad rates at the 95% level for three different populations. They have bad rates of 1%, 3% and 5% and the errors are calculated over a range of sample sizes.

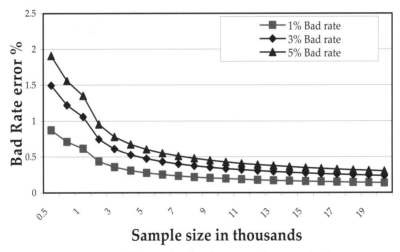

Sample size in thousands

Figure 6.1 Errors by bad rate and sample size

The chart shows that the higher the bad rate of the sample, the higher the error, although proportionately it is less. For 500 cases the error on a 1% bad rate portfolio is almost 1%, whereas for the 3% portfolio it is 1.5%. It is interesting to note that the error curves flatten beyond 10,000. This means that super large samples provide little benefit in terms of accuracy of the model.

Getting more Bads

So when faced with a small sample of Bads, what does the developer do?

Many developers will go back to the sample and look for more Bads. Wait a minute! In chapter 5 we looked at definitions and suggested a rigorous approach to identifying the Bads. At Welbeck Finance in the 1980's the Bad definition was changed to ever more than twice two payments in arrears to increase the number of Bads to 1,500. However it was later discovered that customers who reached this point but did not progress to three in arrears were some of the most profitable!

Another approach is to look outside the sample window to find more Bads. Most commonly these come from recent applications. This means that the Goods and Rejects may have one performance period but the average for the Bads is less. Consider which type of customers become Bad quickly. They will include frauds; there may be customer service and data capture issues; or there may be poor underwriting decisions that should be addressed by improved verification.

In chapter 7 we will look at the robustness of characteristics. The same test can be applied to early Bads. Compare the attributes of early Bads and later Bads. If they are similar then pulling early Bads will be appropriate. However, it is my experience that this is rarely the case and that early Bads should be dealt with differently.

Re-evaluate

If there are not enough Bads for the level of accuracy required, the developer should go back to the business need and question whether a Good:Bad model is appropriate. If there are really so few Bads does the company have a credit quality issue? I was once asked by a company how they could build a model with less than 50 Bads. It turned out that they wanted to increase sales and automate the decisions. The answer was to build an Accept:Reject model. This identified the discrimination between decisions taken by the underwriters. By comparing the 50 Bads with the Rejects and then combining them, the company had a ranking tool that enabled them to increase acceptance rates. The estimate of risk was very inaccurate but at the existing levels it was insignificant and the business could see the trade off between risk and acceptance rates over time.

If the business is adamant that a Good:Bad model is required there are a number of options:
- A generic scorecard
- A tuned scorecard
- A Bayesian Belief (Expert) scorecard

The generic scorecard will be off-the shelf and may be either a bureau scorecard or one built on a similar (undisclosed) portfolio. If the business has other scorecards in operation, tuning an existing scorecard to fit the other population is an option and was affectively achieved for the launch of the GM Card where HFC Bank had no prior credit card experience but had retail portfolios including credit card customers.

The Bayesian Belief approach is basically a derived dataset based on experts' beliefs regarding the different risks. The bad rate for each attribute is expressed as:

$$\text{Bad rate} = (B + b) / (N + n)$$

Where B/N is the bad rate that the experts expect and b/n is the bad rate observed in the small sample. This is not as easy at it seems from the simple equation above. The developer must decide on the relative size of the sample and expert opinion (n/N). There are also decisions about who is involved and how their views are weighted.

Modelling approach

In chapter 8 we will look at modelling techniques. For application scorecards, the technique should be determined by the sample size. Based on typical bad rate we can express this in terms of numbers of Bads. Table 6.1 is a good practice guide to choosing the technique based on the number of Bads in the sample.

Number of Bads	Technique
< 75	Bayesian Belief Scorecard
75 - 150	Weights of Evidence (WOE) Scorecard
150 - 500	WOE's as Characteristics and Linear regression (OLS)
500 - 1500	OLS or Logistic Regression
> 1500	Logistic Regression

Table 6.1 Guide to techniques by number of Bads

Conclusion

Size does matter a great deal when considering the technique and accuracy of the prediction.

Increasing the number of Bads by resampling or redefining the Bad definition is dangerous and ill advised. It is better to question the objective of the model and the required accuracy. It is good practice to calculate the error in predicted bad rate by score band so that the business appreciates the accuracy of the prediction. We will see in chapter 22 that this is vital for the purposes of 'PD' estimation for an Internal Ratings Based (IRB) approach to capital adequacy.

7

Characteristics and Attributes

Distrust the data

Alvin Toffler, the American writer said "You can use all the quantitative data you can get, but you still have to distrust it and use your own intelligence and judgment." In scorecard development the process of evaluating characteristics begins with the summary counts of the data for each variable. This enables the developer to compare the sample with the data definitions, identifying unexpected codes and beginning to understand the nuances of the business.

The review will identify missing data, and failing to set default values for missing data. However, missing data is just one of the issues. The other common types of data preparation error include:

- Deriving characteristics incorrectly
- Failing to ensure data formats and values are consistent with the live environment
- Mis-classifying the Goods and Bads
- Incorrectly weighting the sample to represent the population
- Incorrectly combining customer level data
- Inappropriately augmenting credit reference information

We could build models using continuous data and some industries do. However we rarely have enough data to build robust continuous models. In credit scoring we tend to build standard 'point score' based models, grouping the attributes for each variable to achieve significant groups.

Variables like 'deposit' can have as many alternatives as there are records. So continuous variables usually require 'fine classing' first. Before automatically converting all time-based characteristics into years, the developer should look for clusters and review important breaks with the business. For example, may application forms ask for previous address if time at address is less than 3 years. It is therefore good practice to look at finer intervals around this period to help identify applicants rounding up to hide an address.

In chapter 4 we looked at the statistic known as Information Value. This provides the developer with an indication of the likely contribution a variable will have to a scorecard. At the fine classing stage, the developer is already likely to be excluding variables that have low Information Values. He will also be using the report to highlight outliers and potential problem cases. With agreement from the business, records may be removed from the sample based on outlier codes although these should be the exception. The developer should also be looking for trends and evidence of sub-populations. The latter may require a separate scorecard.

Grouping

The next stage is grouping by combining the low order attributes to produce more robust variables. There is a statistical approach to identifying a significant difference between bad rates of attributes: T-test for differences in proportions. This is a very handy tool to quickly combine attributes, however it is good practice to review the groups rather than automatically accept the grouping.

We'll look at the t-test later. In some countries the developer must also consider any legal requirements. For example in the US, point scores associated with age must progress logically with older applicants scoring more than younger.

Many developers prefer to group attributes by comparing bad rates by eye. A rule of thumb is that there should be at least 50 Goods and 50 Bads in each group and a minimum of 5% of the sample.

Attribute	Goods	Bads	Bad rate
Blank	221	266	54.6%
Not Asked	3	5	62.5%
Retired	40	14	25.9%
No Income	9	10	52.6%
< 1m	2	3	60.0%
1 to 5	106	133	55.6%
6m to 11m	73	87	54.4%
1y to 1y5	82	112	57.7%
1y6 to 1y11	38	51	57.3%
2 y to 2y5	90	89	49.7%
2y6 to 2y11	96	88	47.8%
3y to 4y5	98	98	50.0%
4y6 to 5y5	79	68	46.3%
5y6 to 6y5	62	46	42.6%
6y6 to 7y5	45	38	45.8%
7y6 to 8y5	42	35	45.5%
8y6 to 9y5	23	18	43.9%
9y6 to 10y5	63	46	42.2%
10y6 to 11y11	42	29	40.8%
12y to 14y11	65	32	33.0%
15y to 19y11	77	26	25.2%
20yr to 25y5	41	13	24.1%
25y6 to 99y	37	12	24.5%
99y +	1	1	50.0%
Total	1435	1320	

Figure 7.1 Characteristic Analysis example

The most important rule is that attributes grouped together should be logical. Combining similar bad rates where cell counts are low, will appear to produce a more powerful characteristic but there is always the risk that the result is spuriously high. It is not unknown for characteristics to appear in a final scorecard due to poor grouping rather than any true predictive quality of the variable.

Figure 7.1 is a Characteristic Analysis of 'time in job'. The variable has been fine classed. Records that contain no code ('blank') may be very important. The developer should always ask, how this has occurred. Is the record from a sub-population that didn't require data capture? Is no input a valid result? If the business accepted blanks in the past will they continue to?

The developer should use the Characteristic Analysis to compare the bad rates (or Weights of Evidence), consider cell counts and apply common sense. He may need to investigate:

- application form changes
- code changes
- operator practice (use of a catch all code)

In the example '99' turned out to be used when the field had been validated many years before. Blank was now an acceptable response and would continue to be and so '99' was grouped with 'blank'.

If the developer simply grouped based on bad rate he would consider combining 'blank' and <12 months. 'Not asked' and 'blank' look different, but the code for 'Not asked' was equivalent to 'blank. Again ignoring the low cell counts and common sense, '<1 month' and 'Not Asked' might be grouped, but should not be.

The grouping is shown in the Characteristic Analysis in figure 7.2. All discrete and no answer attributes were combined and investigated later to ensure housewives and retirees seemed to achieve compensatory point scores elsewhere.

Attribute	Goods	Bads	Goods %	Bads %	WoE
No Info	275	297	19.16%	22.48%	-0.16
< 2 yrs	301	386	20.98%	29.22%	-0.33
2yrs to 2yrs11mths	186	177	12.96%	13.40%	-0.03
3yrs to 3yrs11mths	72	82	5.02%	6.21%	-0.21
4yrs to 6yrs5mths	167	131	11.64%	9.92%	0.16
6yrs6mths to 9yrs5mths	110	91	7.67%	6.89%	0.11
9yrs6mths to 14yrs11mths	170	107	11.85%	8.10%	0.38
15years+	154	50	10.73%	3.79%	1.04

Figure 7.2 Characteristic Analysis after grouping

Attribute	Goods	Bads	Goods %	Bads %	WoE
No Info	275	297	19.16%	22.48%	-0.16
< 2 yrs	301	386	20.98%	29.22%	-0.33
2yrs to 2yrs11mths	186	177	12.96%	13.40%	-0.03
3yrs to 3yrs11mths	72	82	5.02%	6.21%	-0.21
4yrs to 8yrs5mths	254	204	17.70%	15.44%	0.14
8yrs6mths to 14yrs11mths	193	125	13.45%	9.46%	0.35
15years+	154	50	10.73%	3.79%	1.04

Figure 7.3 Final grouping

This example serves to illustrate the problem of an illogical progression in Weights. It is likely that the final point scores would increase to 6 years 5 months and then dip for the next group. Whilst there is a significant difference between the bad rates of the two groups, the dip could not be explained. As a result the developer regrouped the attributes to ensure a logical trend in risk.

The t-test

The standard test for differences between bad rates is the t-test, the equation for which is:

$$t = (b_1 - b_2) / \sqrt{(v_1 + v_2)}$$

where b is the bad rate and v is the variance for the attribute. The subscript denotes adjacent attributes. The variance can be estimated (known as the binomial approximation) by

$$v_1 = b_1 \times (1 - b_1)) / (n_1 - 1)$$

where n is the number of Goods plus Bads for the attribute. Table 7.1 illustrates the calculation where attribute 1 is '<2yrs' and attribute 2 is '2yrs to 2yrs11mnths'. The significance is based on the number of degrees of freedom and the level of confidence. Degrees of freedom are calculated by $n_1 + n_2 - 2$. Look up tables are available for the t-test, however as a quick guide, provided the degrees of freedom are more than 20, a t value of more than 2 is significant at the 95% level. In our example, the value is more than 2 and so we can be 95% confident that there is a significant difference between the two groups.

$b_1 - b_2$	v_1	v_2	t
7.4%	0.0004	0.0007	2.2954

Table 7.1 T-test example

Modelling the characteristics

The modelling process removes the correlation between the variables. A simple WoE scorecard takes the weights from the Information Value calculation and transforms them into point scores. The problem with this is double counting of information because variables such as age and time at address are highly correlated.

Figure 7.4 is an example of a score distribution created for a WoE scorecard ignoring correlation. The business assumed the scorecard was separating Goods and Bads exceptionally well –

with two humps: Bads to the left and Goods to the right. The reality was that it was separating young and old applicants because all the younger applicants were also penalised because they were shorter time in job, at their address and with their bank. They were more likely to be renters and had less credit experience.

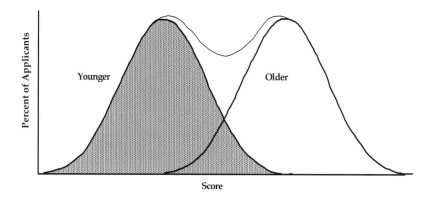

Figure 7.4 Score distribution distorted by double counting

The correlation is graphically illustrated by figure 7.5. Here the circles are equivalent to the Information Values of the characteristics. In the example, half of the predictiveness of 'age' is explained by 'time in job' and 'time at address'.

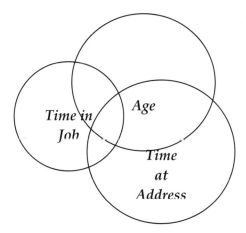

Figure 7.5 Overlap in characteristic information

We will look at modelling techniques that remove correlation in chapter 8, however most developers prefer to use a 'step-wise' approach so that variables can be stepped into the model. In chapter 4 we looked at an interpretation guide for Information Value. As a further rule of thumb, the developer should be cautious where the Information Value is over 0.8. Such characteristics can dominate a scorecard and restrict the influence of a broader range of characteristics. In this situation it is best practice to hold out a dominant variable and step it into the model at a later stage.

Some developers also classify the variables into groups such as:
- Credit bureau
- Reliable
- Unreliable

Unreliable characteristics will be those open to interpretation such as job. Where verification doesn't take place, income is another classic example of an unreliable characteristic. As a result the developer will consider these variables only after all the others have been considered.

Credit bureau variables are sometimes entered into the model as a separate stage so that the business can have a 2 stage scorecard. This is often referred to as a 'residual model'. The difference is that the initial scorecard is fixed, so that the credit bureau variables can not detract from the existing scorecard characteristics.

The benefits of this are that the first stage (no bureau) can be used in a contingency situation; there can be a cut-off at the first stage so that 'superfails' do not go to the credit bureau, thereby reducing bureau costs; should the operation which to switch credit bureau in the future, the first stage of the scorecard can be retained and the scorecard tuned using the new bureau's data as the second stage. Alternatively having the bureau variables as the first stage can produce 'superfails' that are not keyed beyond name and address details, saving operational over head.

Conclusion

Provided the data is legal, use it. The final scorecard will heavily depend on the manipulation of variables and attribute grouping. Because of this, a range of approaches – especially common sense – should be used. The t-test provides a quick method of combining attributes, however too much reliance on automation will result in problems later on. In fact, the developer may find that most of the time spent in the development is checking the validity of data and its interpretation. Remember the Alvin Toffler quote and let intelligence and good judgment be your guide.

8

Modelling Techniques

Regression models

Today, the most common approach to building credit scorecards is to run multiple regression predicting the probability of Good. Figure 8.1 illustrates Ordinary Least Squares (OLS) regression; the 'line of best fit' between variables. The equation for this line is:

$$Risk = \Sigma\, \beta_i\, X_i + c$$

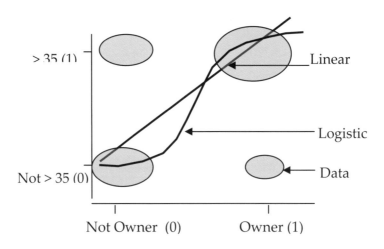

Figure 8.1 Ordinary Least Squares regression for two variables

In the equation, β_i is the correlation coefficient of variable X_i and c is a constant. OLS requires data to be continuous and Normal. Since these requirements are likely to be violated one could argue that this modelling approach should not be used.

Logistic regression, provides a probabilistic solution, more in keeping with the modelling of Good or Bad rates and should produce a more robust solution where sample sizes are reasonable. The scorecard equation is:

$$P(good) \;=\; \frac{Exp(\Sigma\, \beta_i\, X_i + c)}{1 + Exp(\Sigma\, \beta_i\, X_i + c)}$$

where P is the probability and 'Exp' is the exponential function.

The regression equation provides the relationship between the characteristics. In other words, it provides the coefficients that remove the overlap of information. Where dummy (1,0) variables are used the coefficients are the scores prior to any transformation.

In theory Logistic regression should always outperform linear regression, so why do developers continue to use linear regression? Dave Poole Head of Marketing and Risk at IKANO Financial Services can explains this. He says, "we found that there was negligible difference. The logistic regression took longer and linear regression was easier to explain to the business." In addition, there is an issue with the handling of Reject Inference when using Logistic regression. We'll look at this in the next chapter.

Weight of Evidence models
The first credit scorecards were based on the Weights of Evidence. As we have already said, the Weights of Evidence provide a raw score which can then be transformed into integers and an

appropriate range. The Scorecard equation using Weights of Evidence can be expressed as:

$$\text{Score} = \Sigma \, A \, \beta \, (\text{WoE} + c)$$

Where c is a constant applied to each attribute of a characteristic, A is a factor applied to each characteristic and β is the correlation coefficient. The β's are typically found by running a multiple regression on the Weights of Evidence (see chapter 7 to contrast this with using dummy variables). Alternatively the overlap of information between characteristics can be found using a trial and error approach called Iterative Search. The Iterative Search approach is to start with the Weights of Evidence and iteratively step the point scores until the separation of Goods and Bads is maximised. The interative search can be constrained to be linear or non-linear, something we'll discuss in Linear and Non-linear Programming, later in this chapter.

The constant c is often found so that the minimum score for a characteristic is zero. For our Age of applicant example c would be 0.56. When 0.56 is added to each attribute for Age we get the adjusted Weight of Evidence in figure 4.5. This is transformed by the factor A, which may be set to align a scorecard so that a number of points equates to a change in the Odds. We'll look at this in chapter 10.

If the Odds double every 20 points, then A = 28.85. In Table 8.1, the adjusted Weight of Evidence has been multiplied by 28.85. It is important that the same factor is applied to all attributes of characteristics to maintain integrity of the scorecard. The final point score is achieved by applying the correlation coefficient and taking the integer of the result. In Table 8.1 we have assumed that β is 0.5.

A major benefit of Weight of Evidence scorecards is that they can be easily fine tuned. If the factor, A and the correlation coefficients, β are known then any shift in Odds can be directly translated into an adjustment of the point scores.

Attribute	Weight of Evidence	Adj. Weight of Evidence	Scaled (x A)	Point Score
< 25	-0.560	0.000	0.00	0
25 - 34	0.000	0.560	16.16	8
35 +	0.357	0.917	26.46	13

Table 8.1 Adjusting raw scores for the Age example

For example, if the Odds for <25 shift over time become 0.468 then the WoEs have shifted from -0.560 to -0.760, if the shift is uniform throughout all scores, the point score for <25 can be reduced by simple fine tuning.

The new point score is found from the equation:

New Points = Old Points + Aβ (WoE$_{observed}$ - WoE$_{expected}$)

In our example, Aβ is 14.43 so the shift in points is approximately 3 (-0.2 multiplied by 14.43). Note that this approach assumes that the correlations are unchanged and the point scores should be adjusted so that the average score is unchanged (otherwise the cut-off should be adjusted).

Neural networks

Neural networks are widely used for fraudulent transaction detection because of the large amount of available credit card transaction information. However, they are frequently criticised for being 'black-box'. Historically, one major hurdle to neural networks was the difficulty of implementation. In the early 1990's an international bank built a neural network decision system for

Canadian mortgages. It took days to build, but nine months to implement.

Today, vendors appreciate this issue and many provide proprietary software so that the solution is almost 'plug and play'. They also focus on the attraction that neural networks should outperform regression-built scorecards.

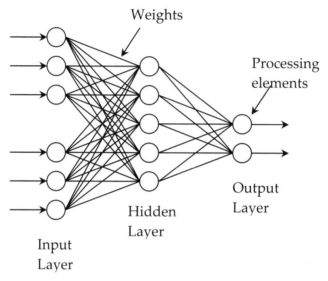

Figure 8.2 A multi-layered neural network

Figure 8.2 illustrates the most commonly applied neural network – the multi-layered perceptron (MLP). Neural net models are nested logistic regression equations. An MLP neural network has an input layer (the variables) and an output layer (risk). The difference between logistic regression and an MLP is that there is also a hidden layer.

A standard credit scorecard will have a single Output node (i.e. Risk or probability of Good). Each hidden layer node is equivalent to a logistic regression, so if we were to have only one hidden layer node, the solution should be as good as the logistic regression model. The benefit of the hidden layer is therefore that it deals with interactions in the data – something that can be solved with regression scorecards only by building multiple scorecards.

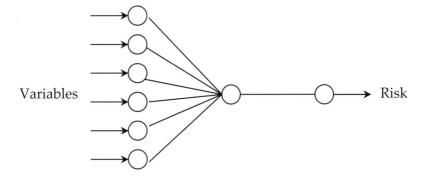

Figure 8.3 A simple neural network

The down side of neural networks is that when applied to in appropriate scenarios, they can over-fit the data, resulting in a model that looks better than it really is. This, along with the black-box complexity and false implication that neural models learn in the operational environment has seen few successful implementation as credit scorecards. However, neural networks should not be dismissed and their power can be used to highlight sub-populations that could lead to separate regression-built scorecards.

Decision Trees
Decision Trees are the organisation of information as a non-recursive partitioning of characteristics available, creating a connected graph with nodes branching into other nodes. The most common technique is CHAID where each partition is identified based on a Chi Squared test on the bad rates of attributes. Figure 8.4 is an example of the first 2 levels of a CHAID analysis.

The first partition is on age over and under 30 since the largest difference in bad rates occurs for this pair of attributes. Subsequent partitions are dependent upon the prior ones, so that for the credit cards split beneath '<30' is based on the bad rates of applicants <30 and with or without credit cards.

The final tree can have numerous nodes. Imagine a scorecard with 10 characteristics each of which has two attributes; a tree to represent the number of alternative combinations would have 1024 nodes (i.e. 2 to the power 10). An issue with Decision Trees is therefore the old one of sample size. To have a tree as effective as a scorecard we would need samples the order of tens of thousands. On the plus side, the final nodes are self explanatory and the user can therefore understand (and explain if necessary) how the decision was arrived at. This is something that traditional scorecards are often criticized for being unable to do.

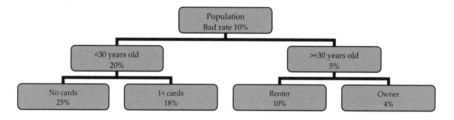

Figure 8.4 Example Decision Tree (truncated)

An alternative to Chi Squared is Information Value and the methodology using this statistic is usually referred to as C4.5. CHAID can be dominated by the size of bad rates, whereas C4.5 is driven by the predictiveness of the variable. It's a subtle difference but one that can make a significant difference in scorecard development. However, due to the sample size constraint, decision trees are rare in the industry with the exception of being used to determine when multiple scorecards are required due to subpopulations or to support scorecards in an explanatory role.

Linear and Non-linear Programming
A Linear Program (LP) is the general term for a problem that optimises an objective function. For scorecards the objective

function may be the Gini coefficient or similar measure of separation. Due to its nature it is also known as 'optimisation theory'. The process typically involves introducing each variable in turn (stepwise) and adjusting the weights (or point scores) to maximise the Gini.

LP constrains the function to be linear. In other words the solution is effectively a trial and error line-of best-fit solution. If the weights of attributes are permitted to be adjusted independently the linear constraint is removed. This is a Non-linear programming (NLP) and was the initial technique employed by Fair Isaac and known as 'Iterative Search'.

Whilst LP and NLP models are lauded for being able to cope with interactions in the data, one of the greatest challenges of NLP is that 'local optima' occur. Think of a myopic mountain climber in a terrain with multiple peaks, and you'll see the difficulty posed for an algorithm that tries to move from point to point only by climbing uphill.

Comparison of techniques

Table 8.2 provides various research results showing the effect of applying different modelling techniques to the same sample. The figures are Gini coefficients, where the higher the Gini the better the discrimination.

Technique Authors	Linear Regression	Logistic Regression	Decision Tree	LP / NLP	Neural Network
Henley[2]	43.4	43.3	43.8	-	-
Boyle[3]	77.5	-	75.0	74.7	-
Srinivsan[4]	87.5	89.3	93.2	86.1	-
Yobas[5]	68.4	-	62.3	-	62.0
Desai[6,7]	66.5	67.3	67.3	-	66.4
Oxley[8]	68.6	68.3	-	-	69.5

Table 8.2 Comparison of model building techniques

There are of course other techniques, ranging from the simple rule based solution, to the highly complex genetic algorithms. As we see from the above table, there is no consistent statistical benefit in using one in favour of another. In fact experienced developers will tell you that it is less about the technique and more about the appreciation of the data.

Conclusion

Occam's razor is a logical principle that states that one should not make more assumptions than the minimum needed. It underlies all scientific modelling and theory building. Scorecard building is no different; it is more about understanding the problem than it is about the specific approach taken. If the power of the scorecard seems incredibly high, then the developer should make sure that the validation sample reflects this performance. Too good to be true often means too good to be true.

The new technologies such as neural networks can be culprits of over-fitting. The issue is not that the techniques are worse, in fact they should be better than regression approaches. The problem is that scorecards need to be understood. In a highly mathematical discipline, the best scorecard may, in fact, be the simplest.

Developers must never forget that the business is more important than the model. There is no point in developing a statistically perfect solution if it is impractical. It must be implementable, understandable and provide business benefits. Statistics can sometimes show an improvement in the discrimination between Goods and Bads, but the benefit is not translated into practice. What matters to the business is acceptance rate, bad rate, processing speed, automation and so on. It is not the Gini coefficient.

9

Reject Inference

The Catch-22

The Swap set is a comparison of a new scorecard with the previous scorecard (or system). The improvement in a new scorecard over the previous one comes from the acceptance of previous Rejects [a] and the rejection of previous Accepts [b]. Table 9.1 shows an example Swap set where the cut off is set ion the new scorecard to achieve the same bad rate as for the old scorecard.

New Scorecard

	Accepts	Rejects	Total
Prior Accepts	48%	12% [b]	60%
Prior Rejects	16% [a]	14%	30%
Total	64%	26%	100%

Figure 9.1 Example Swap set demonstrating improvement

The Catch-22 of scorecard development is that the larger the swap over [a] plus [b], the greater the reliance on reject Inference. In other words, the developers each performed their own estimation of how the prior rejects would have performed. Because of the swap over of past rejects to new Accepts, reject inference is a major contributor to the final power of the scorecard.

However, if it is too aggressive the final scorecard will not perform as predicted.

Trialling scorecards is one way of knowing whether the reject inference is too generous. However, most wise companies will analyse the swap set and take samples of the swapped applications for manual review. We will look at this in the validation of scorecards in chapter 11.

Reject Inference

Reject inference is the process of inferring the performance of accounts that have been rejected. The reason given for this is the 'compensation' for missing information. In other words any scorecard built on accepted accounts only (the Known Goods and Bads) will be biased.

Attributes	Total Sample P(good)	'Accept' Sample P(good)	Reject Risk Ratio
1	0.227	0.446	1.96
2	0.304	0.469	1.54
3	0.314	0.492	1.57
4	0.378	0.552	1.46
5	0.426	0.631	1.48
6	0.556	0.692	1.25

Table 9.2 Example showing the impact of the Rejects

To illustrate the impact of the Reject's attributes on performance, I took an 'Instant Credit' portfolio (with 100% acceptance) and applied an arbitrary cut-off. In this way I would know the true performance of all accounts, but could produce a model as though I didn't know the performance of the artificial 'Rejects'. Table 9.2 illustrates the impact of the Rejects by attribute for a characteristic. There were six attributes, where attribute 1 was the worst (lowest acceptance rate) and attribute 6 was the best. As the likelihood of acceptance increases, the risk decreases (P(good) improves). At the same time the Ratio of the risk (accept P(good) divided by total sample P(good)). This means that the more likely an application is to be rejected, the higher the impact on the bad rate caused by the Reject's attributes.

In simple terms, the less like an Accept, the more we should negatively weight the risk associated with the attributes of the Reject.

Approaches

There is no single, best approach to reject inference (see Hand and Henley[9]). Every developer has his own preferred method of which there are 5 standard approaches:

- Augmentation
- Extrapolation of the Good/Bad prediction
- Matrix multiplication
- Truncation
- Reject referencing
- Graphical

Most techniques infer the performance of the Bads before including them in the development. The generic term for this is 'Parcelling'. The alternative is to exclude the Rejects by augmenting the Known Good Bad population. 'Augmentation' typically involves building a model to separate Accepts and Rejects. The resultant score distribution shows which Rejects are most similar to Accepts. Figure 9.1 is an example comparison.

Table 9.3 shows the Reject distribution broken down into 10 score bands. The ratio of Rejects to the total in each score band is the Augmentation factor applied to the Accepts for the final model build. The extreme Bads (say the worst scoring 5%) tend to have no similar Goods and are often treated as outliers.

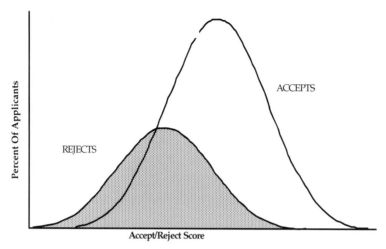

Figure 9.1 Accept and Reject distributions comparison

Score band	1	2	3	4	5	6	7	8	9	10
Accepts	55	199	423	756	981	1213	1647	2251	2547	2312
Rejects	388	412	654	877	1043	913	676	433	201	160
Factor	8.05	3.07	2.55	2.16	2.06	1.75	1.41	1.19	1.08	1.07

Table 9.3 Augmentation factors by score band

In the example, all Accepts in score band 4 of the Accept/Reject scorecard will be counted as 2.16 Accepts in the final scorecard.

Extrapolation is the extension of the Known Good Bad (KGB) model to predict the risk of the Rejects. The Rejects at the same score tend to look as though they would have performed better than the Accept population based on the KGB scorecard. This phenomenon is due to the fact that attributes of the rejects have yet to be weighted into the scorecard. To compensate for this it is best practice to run through the process of predicting the risk and rebuilding the scorecard a number of times.

A common variation on this is for developers to weight the rejects by the inverse probability of acceptance, thus as the application become more likely to be rejected, it become less like the performance predicted by the KGB model.

Matrix multiplication is the combination of two scorecards to predict the reject performance. There are commonly three alternatives for the other scorecards:
- Credit bureau scorecard
- Prior scorecard
- Accept/Reject scorecard

Table 9.4 illustrates a segment of a matrix. One could use the Bad rates from this matrix however, these are the Accepts and at the lowest scores, the lower counts result in larger errors. To compensate for this, developers usually use the estimated Bad rate rather than the actual one. The Bad rate for Rejected applications in cell [a], in Table 9.4, are estimated:

$$[a] = [b] + [b] \times [c] \times n + m,$$

where n and m are constants. m is often set to zero and n set to between 4 and 6. The more the developer wishes to negatively weight the Rejects, the higher the value of n that he will use.

New score Other score	Scoreband 1	Scoreband 2	....	Total
Scoreband 1	11.5% [a]	12.2%	....	8.7%[b]
Scoreband 2	9.6%	8.4%	....	5.3%
Scoreband 3	6.1%	4.9%	....	2.7%
⋮	⋮	⋮	⋮	⋮
Total	6.6%[c]	4.5%	..	0.8%

Table 9.4 Example matrix of bad rates by score bands

In our example, if we use m=0 and n = 6 to estimate the Bad rate of Rejects in the top left hand cell, [a] = 8.7% + 8.7%x6.6%x6 = 12.1%.

So the developer will assign this probability of being Bad to each Reject falling into this cell.

Less scientific approaches

The last three techniques are non-mathematical. The 'Truncation' approach is simply to treat all Rejects as Bad. This is an extreme method that should only be used where a lower acceptance rate is the objective. More commonly this approach is used in conjunction with other techniques, singling out Rejects that the business would never wish to approve. An example of this would be policy decline cases.

'Reject Referencing' is the identification of the Rejected application at the credit bureau to pinpoint the performance of a similar account. Many applicants turned down by one lender are approved by another, thereby providing a pseudo performance for the business that rejected the applicant. However, the developer is faced with an issue of what to do with those whom are not found at the credit bureau. Exclusion of these cases will bias the Reject sample.

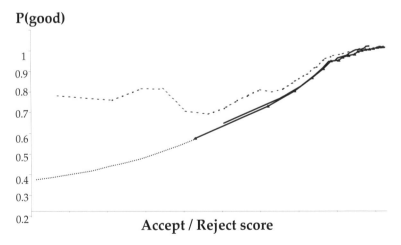

Figure 9.2 Example of fitting the Reject performance by eye

The graphical approach is to take the Known Good Bad score-odds and to plot, by eye, the performance line of the Rejects. Figure 9.2 illustrates this principle where P(good) is the probability of Good calculated for the Accepts and Rejects using the KGB model.

The risk of the Rejects (dotted line) appears to be lower that that of the KGB's. As Poole[10] says, "if we left the Rejects with those probabilities there would be a problem because they are not being properly represented by that Known Good Bad model." The solution is then to judgmentally determine where the line for the Rejects should be. Poole[10] reports that "the technique used by IKANO is to plot the risk of the rejects set by eye. The beauty of this is that you can do it in an Excel spreadsheet, grabbing the points on the graph and moving them down and it will adjust the figures automatically."

Finally there is an alternative to reject inference: approve 'would-be Rejects' for a short period of time so that future scorecards may be built without the need for inference. To be worthwhile, the business requires high volumes to be in this category which in turn means that it is only suitable for high volume businesses since the business is not practically interested in all Rejects, just the ones that are close enough to the current cut-off to be potential swaps in a new scorecard.

Applying reject inference

The outcome of calculating the probability of Good and Bad for the rejects is a decimal. In other words each reject is worth a fraction of Goods and a fraction of Bads. The modelling techniques discussed in chapter 8 have no problem handling these fractions, with one important exception: Logistic regression. This technique relies on binary outcomes - 1 or 0; either Good or Bad. Developers get round the problem by assigning Rejects to either Good or Bad. A common approach is to do this randomly and to check that no bias has occurred. However, this is both risky and unsatisfying. A alternative is to reweight the total sample so that the fractions are multiplied up to become integers. The downside of this is that the number of records is increased by the same proportion, thus resulting in potential processing issues. The treatment of rejects is a significant reason why Logistic regression is not favoured for application scorecard development.

Issues to watch our for

Reject inference is full of issues. If Reject samples are under-represented, the scorecard will be more biased towards the Accepts. The developer must also consider whether there are special categories of Reject. For example policy Rejects should not be treated the same as other Rejects. GE Capital's Cutter (see Bailey[1]) has experienced this problem first hand. "I have had a major vendor build a set of scorecards where they didn't remove a strict policy rule. The resulting scorecards relied heavily of the characteristics of the policy Reject population. The scorecards looked good until we removed the population that should have been excluded!"

There may be characteristics of the Rejects that are under represented by the Accepts. Unless these are considered, they will not appear in a final scorecard simply because there are insufficient records to make the contribution of the attributes significant. In the extreme, imagine all applicants with adverse credit are rejected. The final scorecard will therefore have no adverse credit attributes. This isn't a problem if the business will never accept any one with adverse credit, but if a few cases are allowed, it could be that some bright spark spots that the scorecard doesn't penalise adverse credit and assumes this means the risk is low.

Exaggerated bad performance of the rejects will make the discrimination (Gini) higher. However, near the cut-off, underestimating the risk of the Rejects will result in a larger swap set and bigger improvement for the business. Inconsistent treatment of Rejects may therefore be an indication of manipulation of the results to achieve a bigger, but unrealisable, benefit. GE Capital's Cutter[1] points to the importance of the hold out sample in spotting such issues. "In a recent development (at a previous employer) we found the hold out sample performance to be markedly different from the development sample," he says. "This turned out to be an issue with overly aggressive Reject inferencing!"

Conclusion

Reject inference is more of an art than a science. In this chapter we saw that rejected applications should be considered because their profile will influence the weights associated with the attributes. They may also influence which characteristics enter the scorecard.

The benefit of a new scorecard hinges on its ability to swap Bad previous Accepts for Good previous Rejects. Therefore, the better the swap, the greater the improvement. However, there is a Catch 22 here because the higher the percentage swapped, the less the new Accepts will look like the old known Accept sample.

Whilst a developer must take extreme care inferring the performance of Rejects, a business receiving a new scorecard must do two things: Understand what approach the developer took and how aggressive and consistent they have been, and; Validate the scorecard focusing on the Swap set and where the previous Rejects lie in the new score distribution.

10

Scorecard Alignment

Why align a scorecard?

Scorecard alignment refers to establishing the range of scores appropriate to the perofrmance. Typically this is achieved by setting a point at which the risk is known and the rate with which the risk varies by score. The benefit of aligning the scorecards is so that they can be compared directly with one another without further transformation. This is useful for comparing two populations scored on different scorecards. It is also convenient where accounts progress from scorecard to scorecard; having application and behavioural scores aligned enables an appreciation of how the risk of a customer has varies over time even though different scorecards have been used to assess the score.

Operational benefits of aligning scorecards is that single cut-offs and score ranges, for strategies, can be employed. This provides both consistency and simplicity for system changes and control.

The formulae to align scorecards are discussed in the remainder of this chapter. An alternative, favoured by some developers, is to multiply the output of the regression by a fixed figure (100, for example). The benefit of this approach is that the score can easily be converted back into a Good rate (where P(Good) was the outcome of the model). Of course this is effectively aligning a scorecard, if all scorecards are built and treated the same way. As we will see later, the alignment depends on the sampling and so this simplified approach can be flawed when a sample has been used.

Factor

In chapter 8 we saw that for linear regression, Risk, or P(Good) could be expressed as:

$$\text{Risk} = \Sigma \, \beta_i \, X_i + c$$

where β_i represents the correlation for each variable X_i. In fact the logistic model and Weights of Evidence scorecard can also be manipulated to be expressed such that:

$$\text{Score} = A\Sigma \, (Z_i + C_i)$$

A is a factor applied to all point scores. Z_i is risk estimate, or 'raw score' and C_i is a scalar that is applied to the estimate to provide the required range. We'll look at the scalar next, but for the moment we'll explain A.

A risk estimate can be multiplied by any number to convert it into a number that is considered reasonable. Of course we could have scorecards with probabilities expressed as decimal places. We don't purely because integers are easier to understand, handle and explain. If we factor the distribution, we are changing the spread by an equivalent factor. It might seem that this would invalidate our results, however since we are factoring both the Good and Bad distributions by the same amount, there is no impact on the separation of the distributions; the Gini is unaffected. We can set the factor such that a set number of points equates to a doubling of the Odds. Let's say that

$$A = P / Ln (2)$$

where P is the number of points to double the odds. Fair Isaac typically build scorecard such that for every 20 points (P), the Odds double. In this scenario A = 28.85 (i.e. 20 / Ln2).

Scaling

By adding a constant to our point scores, we effectively change the intercept. In figure 10.1 we can see that adding points merely shifts the distribution to the right. We can therefore use this to set the total number of added points (C = AΣC$_i$) to equate to a predetermined level of risk.

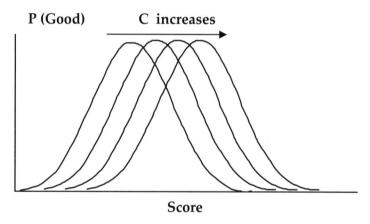

Figure 10.1 The effect of adding a constant

If we want to find C such that 200 points (E) equates to Odds of 30 to 1 (M), and using 20 points double the odds (P) we solve the equation:

$$C = E - P(Ln(M) / Ln (2))$$

In our example therefore C is 101.9 (i.e. 200 – 20xLn30/Ln2). This constant can be added to the final score or allocated to the characteristics. Just how it is allocated doesn't matter, provided that all attributes within a characteristic receive the same number

of points. The resultant Score Odds chart is illustrated in figure
10.2.

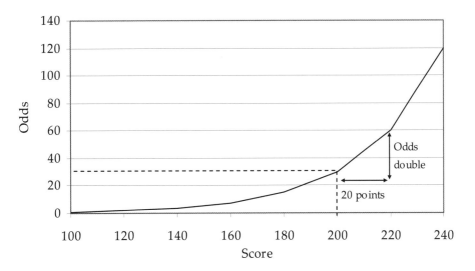

Figure 10.2 Example Score Odds chart

Adjusting for a sample

If the population has been sampled by unequal amounts, the risk
estimate will be based on the Odds of the sample rather than the
population Odds. Whilst this has no effect on the factor, it does
impact the scalar. The equation for finding the constant C which
equates to population Odds M, where the Odds of the sample are
S times that of the population, is:

$$C = E - P(Ln(M) / Ln (2)) - P(Ln(S) / Ln (2))$$

For example, if the Odds of the population are 10 times that of the
sample, then S is 0.1 and C is 35.5 (i.e. 101.9 – 20xLn10/Ln2).

Conversion programs

An easy mistake to make, that I warned of in chapter 1, is to
calculate the scores using these equations and produce the

distributions and statistics. However, most final scorecards are expressed as integers and so the statistics should be based on these scores rather than those calculated with decimal places.

Conclusion

Because of the benefits, most developers choose to align scorecards. Companies receiving scorecards developed by third parties, should ensure that the alignment is to the company's standard rather than that of the developer. If the developer aligns on a different basis, the benefits won't be available.

In chapter 2 we discussed the importance of sampling and understanding the weights of the sample relative to the population. We have seen here that these weights are also important in converting the sample Odds into final Odds for alignment purposes.

11

Scorecard Validation

Textbook statistics

A developer building a scorecard using regression, might think that quoting the R-Squared statistic is enough to provide a validation of the fit of the model to the sample. Unfortunately a high R-Squared value, does not guarantee a good fit to the data. The truth is that the residuals are what are important: how far away are the data from the outcome predicted by the model?

Academics focus on such tools as Graphical Residual Analysis. Different types of plots of the residuals provide information on the adequacy of different aspects of the model. Commonly used numerical methods include the Gini coefficient and the K-S test. However, numerical methods of model validation are narrow, single descriptive variables and better used to determine the discriminatory power of a scorecard rather than a validation tool (we'll look at these in chapter 12).

Hold-out: the true validation

Will the scorecard produce the results predicted by the development sample? This is what we really want to validate. Of course any statistic produced from the development data will be based on the modelling of that data. Practical validation must therefore be more than a single statistic.

The main issue faced by developers is 'Overfitting'. Overfitting is the term used for producing a scorecard that explains the data extremely well, but better than it should. All scorecard developments must be built on a sample and as such are prone to statistical error. Building a perfect predictor based on a small sample is unlikely to produce a good model for predicting the risk of a future sample.

"Although achieving great results on the development dataset is one measure of success, a model highly tuned to a specific dataset will often show great deterioration when implemented on other datasets," says Fair Isaac's Horowitz (reference Bailey[1]). "The model needs to be robust enough to be utilised in the future."

The solution employed by most developers is to have a hold-out sample. A random selection of accounts from the sample that are excluded from the development and subsequently scored using the final scorecard. The statistics of the hold-out sample are then compared with the development statistics.

The hold-out sample tends to be approximately 20% of the original sample. As a rule of thumb, developers like to see at least 500 bads in the hold out sample. This can be a problem if the original sample was short of Bads. Is it better to have fewer Bads in the development so that you can have a reasonable hold out sample or have a reasonable number of Bads in the development? This takes us back to the sample size discussion in chapter 6. It is best practice to determine the required sample size. If there are enough Bads left over, then the developer can consider a hold out sample.

A technique that goes part way towards a hold-out sample is known as 'bootstrapping'. This involves randomly sampling the development sample and whilst this data was used in the development, this subset is also used to produce the scorecard distributions and statistics. Although the bootstrapping approach doesn't show the developer how the scorecard performs on a different sample, it does illustrate the robustness of the scorecard on a smaller subset of the population.

Review the scorecard

Validation is not all about statistics. Sense checks, for example, are also required to ensure that nothing nonsensical has crept into the scorecard. The data coding and crunching has been known to result in embarrassing scorecards.

The most important check is the review of the Characteristic Analysis. The comparison of the development and hold-out sample will also highlight any discrepancies. A Characteristic Analysis of Accepts vs. Rejects will also highlight whether there were significant characteristics associated with the Rejects that should have been considered after the inference process.

The review should also check for 'palatability'; are attributes acceptable for legal, operational, systems and practical purposes? There should be understandable or explainable patterns in the point scores.

Recent sample scoring

Scorecards should also be validated by scoring a recent sample and ensuring the profile, measured by the Stability Index, is similar to that of the development. Scoring a recent sample will also show the Accept and Reject rates the business should expect.

If the business uses underwriters, then a review of cases around the cut-off will provide comfort that the 'swap' seems to be right. Alternatively it may highlight a problem with the scorecard.

If the development has taken a few months, you may find that more recent performance data is available. Ideally the performance period should be the same as that for the development, but shorter will suffice. Applicants from six months prior, could be scored on the new scorecard and their performance compared. Whilst the predicted bad rate will be different from the recent sample, the business may be able to forecast the bad rate over a longer period. The validation exercise will also check that the bad rates decrease as the score increases.

Swap set

There are two types of Swap set. In chapter 9 we looked at the swap of Accepts and Rejects for the new scorecard compared with the current one. The second type is to look at the Goods and Bads separately. Figure 11.1 is an example Swap set for Goods alone at the same acceptance rate.

New Scorecard

Goods	Accepts	Rejects	Total
Prior Accepts	68%	4% [b]	72%
Prior Rejects	14% [a]	11%	25%
Total	82%	15%	100%

Figure 11.1 Example Swap set for Goods

In this example 25% of the Goods were rejected in the development sample. Setting the same acceptance rate, the new scorecard only rejects 15% of the Goods. The Swap set doesn't give the whole picture, but does provide a warning if the swap over is large. As a rule of thumb, a swap ([a] + [b]) of over 20% should be investigated. A large swap will be likely for a first scorecard. Replacing scorecards where scoring has been commonplace for many years will produce much smaller swaps.

We'll talk about trialling the scorecard later. In the meantime, it is good practice to analyse the Swap set and take samples of the swapped applications for manual review.

The most sensitive area is the overrides i.e. accounts underwriters have decisioned contrary to the previous score. This means that there is typically information about the application that the previous scorecard did not evaluate. If overrides are significant, their inappropriate treatment will distort the out turn of the scorecard. Previous rejected overrides may look like previous Accepts and could be scored highly in the new scorecard. Conversely, 'cherry-picked' score-fails (overrides to accept) can imply that Rejects look similar to the overriden cases will score higher using the new scorecard.

A close look at the swapped overrides is therefore advisable as is a review of the reject inference.

Score distribution

To provide an indication of the impact of the Reject Inference, the Accepts and Rejects should be plotted separately as score vs. odds. This will show graphically how the Rejects have been treated around the cut-off and at the lowest scores. A high separation can be achieved by exaggerating the risk of the lowest scorers whilst the performance improvement will be higher the closer the Rejects at the cut-off are to the Accepted accounts.

As we saw in chapter 9, there is no right answer to the inference of the performance of the Rejects. The fewer accounts that are approved, the more important the attributes of the Rejects are.

It should also be remembered that the only area in which Reject inference matters is around the cut-off. The validation should therefore focus on this area.

Where overrides are significant, in addition to the Swap set, the validation should include the new score distributions of both types of override, and a score vs. odds analysis of the overrides.

Challenge the scorecard

Scorecards don't need to be implemented in a fell swoop. A scorecard can be run in parallel for a period of time. This approach is often used when scorecards are implemented for the first time and underwriters are allowed to get used to them. Of course the other side of this is that first scorecards are prone to many issues not least of which is the data they were developed with is often only part of the picture viewed by the underwriters.

GE Capital's Cutter[1] believes that scorecards should be challenged, like any credit strategy. His view is that it is "better to be cautious than risk a disaster for benefit of a bigger gain. We trial the scorecards as champion/challengers and can therefore compare the accuracy of the reject inference."

Because of the swap over of past rejects to new Accepts, Reject inference is a major contributor to the final power of the scorecard. However, if it is too aggressive the final scorecard will not perform as predicted.

Conclusion

"Whilst academics and other statisticians continue to extend and improve modelling technologies, lenders have to realistically assess the costs and benefits associated with increasing model sophistication and investing in more complex validation techniques" (reference Burns and Ody[11]). This was the view from an academic seminar on validation. However, practical validation approaches and common sense are more informative and beneficial that statistical tests.

Validation is vital to identify mistakes made in the development process or scorecards that appear predictive, but will be inadequate for the recent through-the-door business. The receiving business should review the output from the development and ensure that it has been rigorous and in line with the objectives, culture and needs of the business. The score distributions should be checked and particular attention paid to the Reject inference and overrides around the proposed cut-off.

A scorecard can be run in parallel or as a challenger and should be used to score a recent sample to check the stability. If possible a more recent sample with performance will give an early indication of the scorecard's ability to rank.

If the validation identifies any possible issues with the development, it should be corrected. As we saw in the best practice scorecard development process (chapter 2), the developer should be prepared to revisit any stage. If the issue can be corrected, the developer should redevelop. If the scorecard is unsuitable, for example the population has changed significantly, throw the new scorecard away. It is better to start the process again than implement a bad scorecard.

86

12

R-Squared, Gini and Scorecard Power

R-Squared

The fit of a regression line to the data is described by R-Squared: the sum of the squares predicted (SSR) divided by the sum of the squares to the data (SST). Figure 12.1 illustrates these relative distances to the regression line, the standard equation of which was provided in chapter 8.

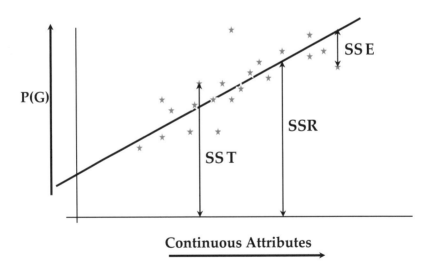

Figure 12.1 Illustration of linear regression distances

The smaller the variability of the residual values (E) around the regression line, the better the prediction. A perfect prediction (SSE = 0) will yield an R-Squared of 1. In the other extreme, if there is no fit to the data, the R-Squared will be zero. The benefit of R-Squared is that the result can be easily interpreted. An R-Squared of 0.6 means that the scorecard has explained 60% of the variability.

As we said in the previous chapter, R-Squared is not a satisfactory measure of the validity of a model. To interpret the statistic the modeller must also understand the residual errors (SSE). In fact, maximising R-Squared can have the effect of increasing the residual errors (see for example Annis[12]).

Divergence
The first measure used by Fair Isaac was Divergence. Where Divergence is measured as:

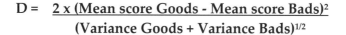

$$D = \frac{2 \times (\text{Mean score Goods} - \text{Mean score Bads})^2}{(\text{Variance Goods} + \text{Variance Bads})^{1/2}}$$

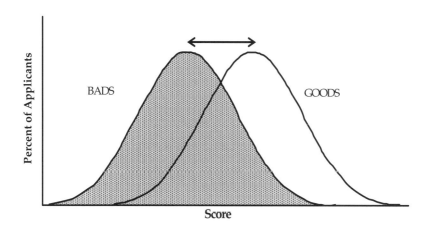

Figure 12.2 Divergence: a measure of separation

The beauty of Divergence is its basis on Normal probability theory. It is effectively the standard error of the difference between two Normal distributions. The factor of two provides a figure that represents the 95% confidence level. However, because of the theory, the measure only works well for distributions that *are* Normal. Another influence is that the variances of the two distributions should be similar. The more dissimilar the spreads of the Goods and Bads, the less reliable the statistic.

As a rule of thumb, an achieved model Divergence in excess of 1 was considered to be a reasonable scorecard.

K-S
The Kolmogorov-Smirnov (K-S) test is another that is supported by statistical tables and found great favour in the 80's and 90's due to its simplicity. It is the maximum separation of the two cumulative distributions.

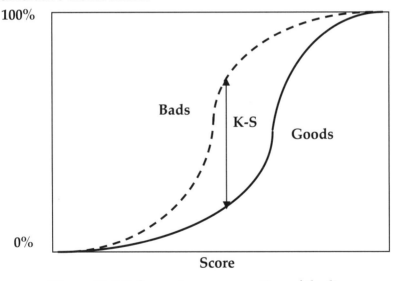

Figure 12.3 K-S: maximum separation of the lines

The statistical tables show that K-S doesn't have to be very large to be significant. For example, with 100 equal score bands the statistic is significant if greater than 14% at the 95% level.

The downside is that K-S is a measure at the maximum separation point only. An extreme problem I once saw was a reasonable K-S, but the distributions were so non-Normal that they crossed over a number of times. In other words at certain points the scorecard predicted the Bads were better than the Goods. A couple of suggested solutions to this issue are:

- Measure the separation at the expected cut-off
- Look at the separation for the bottom 20% and top 20%.

In comparing the discrimination of two scorecards, we find another issue with the K-S graphs: they are score dependent. If we overlay two scorecards, they have to have been aligned for the comparison to be useful. Graphs of the Gini coefficient, on the other hand, don't have this problem.

Gini
The Gini graph is a plot of the cumulative Good s against the cumulative Bads as illustrated in figure 12.4.

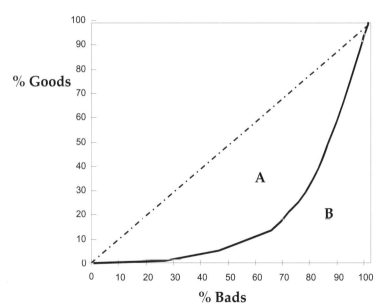

Figure 12.4 An example Gini graph

Gini has become the industry standard measure of the separation of Good and Bad distributions. In the graph, the solid line is the model and the dotted line represents the line of no discrimination (random). K-S is the maximum separation of the two lines. For Normal distributions, K-S tends to be about 80% of the Gini.

In the graph, Gini is the proportion that area A (between the lines) represents. It can be calculated as a coefficient as a ratio of the areas A/(A+B) or 1 – 2B since A is ½. Gini ranges from 0% to 100%, although the percentage sign is often dropped.

An easy way of calculating the area is to break it down into triangles (Within) and squares (Between). Figure 12.5 illustrates this for a simple scorecard.

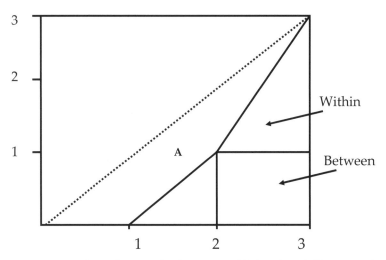

Figure 12.5 Simple graph showing 'Within' and 'Between'

There are 3 Goods and 3 Bads ranked (0,1 ; 1,1 ; 2,1). The calculation for Gini using Within and Between:

Gini = (1 – 2x(Sum(Within) + Sum(Between)) / (CumG x CumB))

Where CumG is the total number of Goods and CumB is the total number of Bads. From the graph in figure 12.5 it can be seen that Within total 1.5 (0.5 + 1) and Between is 1. So in this example the Gini is 44.4% (i.e. 1 - (3+2)/9).

Gini for characteristics

In chapter 4 we looked at Information Value as a measure of the power of a characteristic. Because Gini doesn't rely on a score it can also be used for measuring the power of characteristics. The only pre-requisite is that the attributes are ranked by bad rate prior to the calculation. Let's take a look at the Age of applicant characteristic again, this time calculating the Gini.

Attribute	Goods	Bads	Within	Between
< 25	400	700	140000	0
25 - 34	500	500	125000	200000
35 +	600	420	126000	378000
Total	1500	1620	391000	578000
			Gini:	**20.25%**

Table 12.1 Example Gini calculation for Age

In this example the Gini is 20.25% (i.e. 1 - 2(391000 + 578000) / (1500 x 1620).

Gini depends on sampling

The Gini will change if the sample weights are adjusted. This means that if a scorecard is developed on a sample that is an equal number of Goods and Bads the resultant scorecard Gini will change when the proportions of Goods and Bads are changed to reflect the population.

Typically the developer wants as many Bads as possible so all Bads are used and the Goods may be sampled. An example of the effect of sampling is the scorecard developed with equal sample sizes produced a Gini of 36%. However, when the results were adjusted to reflect that the sample was only 10% of the Goods, the Gini fell to 31.7%. A shocking impact if you are not expecting it and another reason why the developer should take great care in ensuring the population weights (factors) are known.

Rejects can have the greatest impact on the Gini. Figure 12.6 is a Gini graph for 3 scenarios. The first (solid line) is the Accepts only. The second (dotted line) is where the Rejects are not factored. The third (square markers) is where the number of Rejects are doubled.

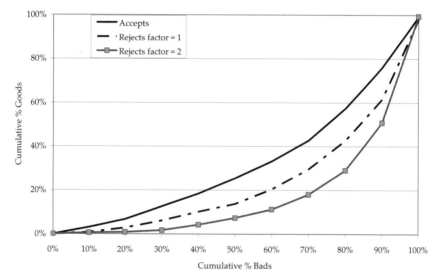

Figure 12.6 Gini graph showing alternative scenarios.

Remember this is a single scorecard. All that has happened is the contribution of the Rejects has been changed by weighting them. The Gini for the three scenarios is 33.2%, 36% and 38.5% respectively. Another good reason for the receiving business to check the Reject inference: the more Rejects the developer assumes, the better the Gini will be.

Acid test

Of course the issue with all these measures is that they are just statistics. What really matters to the business is the trade-off between risk and reward. In other words, the acid test of any scorecard is the bad rate by acceptance rate. In comparing the current and proposed scorecard, what are the bad rates at the same acceptance rate and what are the acceptance rates at the same bad rates?

Let's say the objective of the business is to increase acceptance rates. The new scorecard has a larger Gini, but the acceptance rate for the proposed cut-off maintaining the risk is worse. In this situation the larger Gini is irrelevant.

Conclusion

The statistical measures we have looked at here are useful relative guides to the power of a scorecard. The most popular today is Gini because of its versatility and measurement over the whole distribution rather than at a single point as for K-S.

The true test of benefit must come back to meeting the objectives of the scorecard build. If it is about improving the accept-bad rate decision, then the improvement in the acceptance rate or bad rate must be checked.

The statistical measures are influenced by the modelling process and we looked at how Gini is affected by the weighting of the sample. This is especially true for the Rejects and so the validation must include a check of the factors used to ensure accuracy and the Reject inference to ensure reasonableness – especially around the cut-off and the extremes.

13

Scorecard Monitoring

Change happens

Monitoring a scorecard is effectively continuing the validation. Foley of Crif says, "Some organisations still think they can implement scoring without monitoring its performance on an on-going basis. But fixing a poor credit system is like turning an oil tanker at sea; it'll carry on for miles in the same direction before it turns around" (reference Bailey[1]). Monitoring ensures that early warning signs are spotted so that the business can respond either by tuning their decisions or by redeveloping the model. Monitoring is also a good discipline since it helps the analysts understand the strengths and weaknesses of the models.

One of the principles of scoring is that the future is like the past. But populations change. Overtime there are trends that change the characteristic mix of the portfolio even if they are effectively the same applicants. This socio-demographic evolution is particularly important for credit scoring as, over time, more and more people get credit, have a greater number of credit cards and increase cross-product holdings. Other trends are for greater home ownership, shorter time at address and shorter bank account relationships.

Other than economic changes there are also the ones driven by the operation or marketing. Geographic expansion occurs for many lenders. For example a building society may start in one region of the country with a very specific, local market. Overtime though expansion and acquisition, the society may find themselves lending nationally. Applicants in new areas may be quite different from those that the finance company is used to underwriting. Marketing has a major impact on the applicant population. A change in promotion of a product can attract different customers. A store card operation that switches to a 5% initial discount will see an improvement in profile as customers who would have paid by other means switch to the store card due to the financial offer. There are two effects that this change can have: 1. The scorecard will correctly predict the risk but the risk will change due to the shift in the distribution, or 2. The scorecard will predict badly because the population is different from the one used to build the scorecard. Monitoring is therefore critical to the success of a scorecard. Implementing a scorecard without monitoring would be like launching a submarine without sonar.

Decision monitoring

Monitoring new business usually involves reporting on key figures, for example:

- Acceptance rate
- Override rates
- Average application score
- Average acceptance score
- Average bureau score

All of these provide indicators of the profile for comparison with previous periods. Using the score distribution, one can also measure the similarity between this period's and the development sample. The most common measure of this is Stability Index where the separation of the observed and expected (development) is measured over a range of score bands. Similar measures include the K-S and Chi-Squared tests. Each of these is testing the significance of the difference between the two distributions. Secondly, the characteristics of the population can be compared. Typically these are the ones used in the scorecard, but it is recommended that other key characteristics are tracked. For example channel, source or terms may be important in identifying sub-populations whose mix contributes significantly to the overall performance. Portfolio monitoring can also be achieved by reviewing a 'Final Score Report'. This report provides details of numbers and percentages accepted and rejected for each score and hence the level of overrides compared to the cut-off. It should also provide the number and the percentage of accounts decisioned without scoring.

Population stability

The distribution of observed applications, provides an early test of the assumption that the present is like the past. Even without performance information, it is likely that if the observed distribution is significantly different from the expected, the performance of the scorecard and/or the portfolio will not be as expected. It is advisable to test a new scorecard against recent applications to identify whether there has been a shift in the population since development and, at the same time, test for scorecard coding errors.

Figure 13.1 shows a summary of the percentage falling in each score band, comparing the expected with the observed. Typically the report will also show the number of applicants, the number of acceptances and the acceptance rate for each score band of the scorecard. Here we have demonstrated the calculation of the Stability Index, the most common measure of population stability. The equation for this is:

$$\text{Stability Index} = \Sigma[(A - B) \times Ln(A/B)] \times 100 \%,$$

where A is observed percentage at each score band. B is the expected (development) and this is totalled over all score bands.

score band	Expected % Applications	Observed % Applications	0%-E%	LN(0%/E%)	SI
< 172	3.0%	2.5%	-0.5%	-18.2%	0.1%
173 - 181	4.0%	7.1%	3.1%	57.4%	1.8%
182 - 189	5.0%	4.8%	-0.2%	-4.1%	0.0%
190 - 197	3.5%	3.9%	0.4%	10.8%	0.0%
198 - 205	8.0%	3.7%	-4.3%	-77.1%	3.3%
206 - 213	8.5%	4.4%	-4.1%	-65.8%	2.7%
214 - 221	11.3%	7.3%	-4.0%	-43.7%	1.7%
222 - 229	9.6%	10.1%	0.5%	5.1%	0.0%
230 - 237	8.6%	10.2%	1.6%	17.1%	0.3%
238 - 245	11.0%	12.3%	1.3%	11.2%	0.1%
246 - 258	13.5%	18.2%	4.7%	29.9%	1.4%
259 - 270	14.0%	15.5%	1.5%	10.2%	0.2%
	100.0%	100.0%			**11.7%**

Figure 13.1 Extract from a Population Stability Report

Generally, the interpretation of Stability Index is:

Stability Index	Stability	Interpretation
Less than 10%	No change	OK
10% to 24.9%	Slight shift	Caution
25% and above	Shift	Danger

Table 13.1 Stability Index interpretation guide

It is best practice to have between 10 and 20 bands and approximately the same proportion of expected applications in each. To simplify programs, analysts often set the score bands at regular intervals. However, this results in high proportions in the middle score bands and low percentages at the extremes. Note that this will have the effect of making the measure more sensitive to changes at the extremes rather than reflecting the overall shift.

Before we look at the types of shift, remember that even if there is instability in the score distribution, the scorecard may still be ranking risk – although it is unlikely to be optimal. Stability Index is a warning metric and shouldn't be used on its own.

Types of shift

In the example above, the Stability Index is 11.7%. This suggests there has been a shift that should be investigated. However, this does not tell us where the problem is or what it is. There are three categories of population shift:

- Parallel
- Cross-over, and
- Kinked

A Parallel shift is where the average score shifts up or down, but the spread of the distribution is unchanged. This type is the least concerning. Typically it represents the same population impacted in some way. The shift in demographics, with credit card holders holding an increasing number of credit cards would cause a shift in the score of people based on number of credit cards.

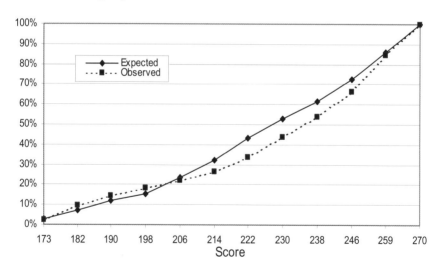

Figure 13.2 Example cumulative score distributions

A Cross-over means that the spread of the distribution has changed and when the cumulative distribution is plotted, the curves will intersect. This type of shift is usually indicative of a serious problem. If the distribution is narrower then the separation of the Goods and Bads must be worse. If the distribution is wider, then questions should be asked about the accuracy of the expected distribution or the influence of sub-populations.

A Kinked distribution is a non-linear cross-over and is indicative of a scoring problem. Typically there is either a scorecard error or there is manipulation. Figure 13.2 shows the distribution plotted cumulatively. A cross-over occurs in the score band 198-205, however the distribution is Kinked with a bulge of applications scoring above the cut-off of 190. This is a Motor finance portfolio where underwriters are used to work with the dealers to find terms appropriate to the car purchaser. So the analyst should look at the distribution as well as the statistics to determine whether further analysis and action is required.

Characteristic analysis

The Stability Index can identify that there has been a significant shift, but it doesn't pinpoint the problem. Overall, it might tell us that applicants are scoring higher. It does not say how much higher they are scoring, nor does it tell us the reason. It could also mask an issue if there are compensating errors: if the average scores were the same, for example, there could be a negative shift for one characteristic that is cancelled out by a positive shift for another. We can therefore look at the average score for each characteristic and compare that for the Expected and Observed populations.

Table 13.2 is an example Average Score report demonstrating the contribution of each scoring characteristic to the overall shift in average scores. In this example the average score has increased from 159.4 to 170.8. The report shows that the biggest shift has come from answers to the Telephone question which has contributed to 5.7 points. The only decrease comes from Searches which has contributed by -0.8 points on average.

Chracteristic	Expected	Observed	Score Difference
Age	3.1	3.7	0.6
Marital Status	5.9	6.7	0.8
Dependants	11.8	11.9	0.1
Residential Status	15.8	16.6	0.8
Telephone	39.0	44.7	5.7
Time at Address	4.8	5.4	0.6
Tim in Job	9.4	11.5	2.1
Credit Reference	59.9	61.4	1.5
Searches	9.7	8.9	-0.8
	159.4	170.8	11.4

Table 13.2 Example Average Score report

Attribute	Exp %	Obs %	Difference	Points	Shift
Yes	81.70%	92.70%	11.00%	52	5.72
No	18.30%	7.30%	-11.00%	0	0
	100%	100%			5.72

Table 13.3 Example Characteristic Analysis report

Table 13.3 shows where these figures come from. If we take Telephone, there are two attributes 'Yes' and 'No'. 11% more people are providing a telephone number. Since the score awarded to 'Yes' in our example is 52, on average the increase is 11% times 52.

The advantage of the Characteristic report is that it can pinpoint the cause. It can not identify a cause that is not in the scorecard and so key characteristics of potential sub-populations should also be monitored. The analyst may also use a mixture of statistics and we recommend that Chi-Squared is used in conjunction with average scores. Chi-Squared may identify a significant shift in attributes that have low point scores particularly where other attributes have compensating, but smaller percentage shifts.

Dynamic delinquency

Performance should be monitored by cohort of new business. In this way the analyst can relate the acceptance decision with the risk and hence link it back to the expected performance.

A Dynamic Delinquency Report is illustrated in figure 13.3. The vertical dates are the months the accounts were booked. The column heading dates relate to the month the performance is observed. The cells in the table are the proportion of accounts which are Bad within that particular month.

	Jan-01	Feb-01	Mar-01	Apr-01	May-01	Jun-01	Jul-01	Aug-01
Pre-01	7.50	7.50	7.50	7.50	7.50	7.50	7.50	7.50
Jan-01		0.40	2.16	3.88	5.06	5.70	6.50	7.14
Feb-01			0.40	2.16	3.88	5.06	5.70	6.50
Mar-01				0.40	2.16	3.88	5.06	5.70
Apr-01					0.45	2.43	4.37	5.69
May-01						0.45	2.43	4.37
Jun-01							0.40	2.16
Jul-01								0.40

Figure 13.3 Example Dynamic Delinquency Report

For scorecard monitoring, the Bad definition is ideally that used in the scorecard development. However other arrears definitions can be used, particularly where and earlier arrears definition is required as an early warning. Dynamic delinquency reports tend to be used more for portfolio tracking and forecasting than for the evaluation of the scorecard. The later is better achieved by the Characteristic Odds Report and Score-Odds.

Characteristic Odds

In the same way the Characteristic Analysis Report monitored the proportions of application by each attribute of a characteristic, the Characteristic Odds Report compares the performance of each attribute. Table 13.4 is an example for the characteristic 'Credit cards'. It firstly illustrates the need to look at the Information Odds rather than bad rates since the overall bad rate is different. There has been a significant shift in the risk associated with 'MasterCard'. In chapter 8 we considered Weight of Evidence scorecards. The information provided by the shift in Information Odds enables the analyst to fine tune the point scores associated with the attributes.

Attribute	Expected Bad rate	Observed Bad rate	Expected Info Odds	Observed Info Odds
None/NA	7.27%	8.23%	0.72	0.72
MasterCard	4.25%	4.11%	1.27	1.50
Visa	5.67%	7.18%	0.94	0.83
M/C + Visa	4.15%	4.78%	1.30	1.28
	5.3%	6.0%	17.73	15.54

Table 13.4 Example Characteristic Odds Report

The downside is that the observed performance should be at the same Performance period as that used for the scorecard development which may mean a long wait. A compromise is therefore to track the performance earlier and forecast the bad rates for a direct comparison of the risk.

Score-Odds
The comparison of the observed vs. the expected performance by score is the ultimate test of a scorecard. To obtain a graph that is easier to interpret, analysts usually plot the natural log of the odds (Ln(odds)) against score. An example is shown in figure 13.5. Here we see that the Observed performance differs from that of the development statistics. The score bands 370-390 have worse than expected performance. Below 370 the performance is the same or better than expected. It is more common to see performance deteriorate by score although <350 is explained by cherry picking

by underwriters. The score band 360-369 is not so easily explained.

The degree to which the scorecard is misaligned can be measured by what we call the 'Misalignment Index'. This measures the relative shift in odds between the observed and expected performance. Alternatively measures like Gini are used to illustrate the deterioration in discrimination.

Having identified a misalignment overall, the analyst should identify the characteristic(s) causing the shift. For this we use the same measure, since the alignment should be independent of the attributes.

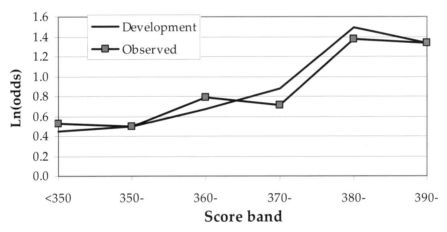

Figure 13.5 Example Score-odds graph

Characteristic misalignment

The Misalignment Index is the sum of each 'Odds Index' multiplied by the proportion of accounts in the score band.

The Odds Index is the positive solution of the natural log of the ratio of the Information odds observed and the Information odds expected. i.e.

| Ln(Info Odds(observed)/ Info Odds(expected)) |

Table 13.5 is an example of this calculation in action. The characteristic is 'Credit cards held' and the attribute is '1+ cards'. Here we see that the misalignment tends to increase with score; using the proportion of accounts weights the index so that lower proportions have a lesser impact on the measure.

Population Odds = 50:1	1+ Credit Cards				
Scoreband	Accept Prop.n	Interval Odds (E)	Interval Odds (O)	Odds Index	MI
<350	6.8%	0.45	0.53	0.16	1.1%
350-359	7.5%	0.50	0.50	0.0	0.0%
360-369	10.0%	0.67	0.79	0.16	1.6%
370-379	10.0%	0.88	0.71	0.21	2.1%
380-389	11.2%	1.09	1.38	0.24	2.6%
390+	54.2%	1.34	1.44	0.07	3.9%
	100%	Misalignment Index:			11.3%

Table 13.5 Example Misalignment Report

As a rule of thumb, a Misalignment Index of more than 20% indicates a serious problem that most likely requires redevelopment rather than tuning of the scorecard.

Sub populations

So far we have considered reporting at the total portfolio level. Alternatively the reports can be produced by product, by branch or region, by source of business or at a sub-population level. For example, one may split the analysis by the amount borrowed. This may be important to the business since the scorecard is assessing numbers of Goods and Bads rather than balance at risk. Therefore if the Odds look right, but the Bad accounts have borrowed more than the Good accounts, the Odds expressed as balances will be worse. This will have big implications for profitability.

Conclusion

Tracking is a vital element of using a scorecard. Initially the tracking is about the decisions and the stability of the population. As performance builds up, we are able to look at the characteristic odds and compare the expected and observed performance.

It is best practice to analyse the performance of the scorecard by removing the overall risk (i.e. use Information Odds) otherwise a discriminating scorecard in a deteriorating environment will look like it is losing power. We'll look at this again in chapter 21.

Dynamic delinquency is a staple for tracking, but to evaluate whether the scorecard is working optimally, the analysis must be by score. Gini can be tracked but is again a single dimension. Better analysis is at the score band level and the score-odds graph will provide a simple way to eye-ball the alignment of the scorecard. A measure like the Misalignment Index we use, will enable a quick calculation to find problem characteristics and should be taken to the attribute level to identify fine tuning opportunities.

Finally, scorecard tracking can be a full time occupation. It shouldn't be. The principle should be to analyse only what appears to be an issue. Start at the highest level and drill down into the data where variances are observed.

14

Scorecard or Other Problems

Is it the scorecard?

If the delinquency is out of line with that predicted, the first assumption is often that the scorecard is to blame. A problem with the scorecard is only one of many possibly causes. Problems are rarely simple. In fact a good golden rule is that if the problem seems easy, look again. The hardest part of any problem is often to pinpoint the true issue. Statistical tests do not do this, they merely support the findings.

The non-scorecard problems are many, but will typically include:
- Fraud
- Policy rule changes
- Lending limit or credit limit changes
- Collections strategy changes
- Override and other underwriting activity
- Product changes
- Accounting policy changes
- Cross-sell activity
- Pricing changes
- Third party/intermediary treatment

And of course there are the factors the lending organisation has no control over: the economy and the direct competition.

Problem solving tools involve symptom identification. One of the most effective is to ask "What don't we know about the problem?" Another is to map out events over time: a chronological analysis. This may enable the analyst to link cause and effect. Other tools include: maps such as Mind and Tree maps; Fishbone analyses, and; Force field analyses to identify what strengthens and weakens the problem.

Score profile analysis

Application profile monitoring was covered in chapter 12. The scorecard analyst must watch for an impact on the expected risk caused by a shift in population. A lower profile of the same population will mean an adjustment is required to the Expected risk. A different population may mean a breakdown of the scorecard's ability to discriminate. In other words, the latter is a problem whereas the former may be a symptom requiring no action other than to change predicted outcomes for later analyses.

The first indicator of a shift may be the Stability Index. A shift of more than 0.1 (see Appendix v) is worthy of further investigation. A general upwards or downwards shift in the distribution will typically mean that there is less concern about the scorecard itself. Where the distribution becomes wider or narrower (described as Cross-over, because when plotted cumulatively the Observed and Expected lines cross) further investigation is required.

A third type of shift can occur, namely non-linear. This will often relate to either a dramatic change in applicant population or a kink typically caused by either: Manipulation of the applications due to outside knowledge of the scorecard or a bias caused by the application form design. Clearly, these are best resolved at the source, but it could be that a sub-population, insignificant in the development, has become a significant variable. Figure 14.1 is an example of a motor finance scorecard distribution, where 'negotiation' with the dealers has resulted in a distribution with a dip below the cut-off of 40 and a bulge just above it.

If the distribution is kinked, try and understand where the problem is and why. Manual review of applications will help this process. If the shift has not been caused by a system error or manipulation, consider a sub-population. If this is the first analyses of the application profile, check that the expected distribution was correct.

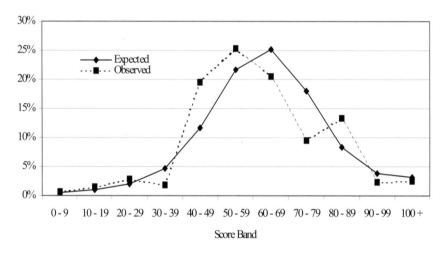

Figure 14.1 Example of a Kinked distribution

Characteristic: Instalment

	Exp	Obs	Difference	Points	Shift
< £100	6.2%	13.6%	7.4%	16	1.18
£100 - £139	30.4%	38.2%	7.8%	13	1.01
£140 - £179	29.1%	28.1%	-1.0%	9	-0.09
£180 +	34.3%	20.1%	-14.2%	0	-

Total		100.0%	100.0%		Average	2.11

Figure 14.2 Example Average Score analysis

The Average Score Report (chapter 13) will highlight score shifts. These should be investigated where average shifts are significant.

Figure 14.2 is an example illustrating the points shift for each attribute, calculated by the difference in proportion multiplied by the point score of the attribute. Average scores are however, by there nature, biased by the point scores. Chi-Squared (see Appendix ii) is not and will provide the analyst with a better measure of significant changes in the mix of attributes because it is independent of the score.

The Chi-Squared test (e.g figure 14.3) may highlight characteristics that would not have otherwise been investigated. They should lead the analyst to question whether a sub-population is the cause of the change in distribution. Sub-populations are typically those that require a separate scorecard and could be based on:

- Age of applicant
- Age of vehicle
- Application channel
- Credit product
- Client/Retailer group

Characteristic: Instalment

	Exp	Obs	Chi Sq
< £100	6.2%	13.6%	8.8%
£100 - £139	30.4%	38.2%	2.0%
£140 - £179	29.1%	28.1%	0.0%
£180 +	34.3%	20.1%	5.9%
Total	100.0%	100.0%	16.7%

Figure 14.3 Example Chi-Squared analysis

The analyst should look at the Stability Index for the sub-population and can test the weakness of the scorecard by calculating an Interaction Index. Interaction is the overlap of information between variables that is not consistent for all variables within the characteristic. The calculation is always based on a 2 x 2 matrix of the odds and needs to be repeated for all pairs of variables where there are more than 2 attributes in the characteristic:

Interaction Index = |LN(Odds$_{11}$ x Odds$_{22}$ / Odds$_{12}$ x Odds$_{21}$)|

Figure 14.4 shows the matrix of Odds where Odds$_{11}$ = 0.85, Odds$_{22}$ = 0.88, Odds$_{12}$ = 0.26, and Odds$_{21}$ = 1.53. In this example the Interaction Index = 0.63. There are no statistical tables for this measure, but as a rule of thumb an Index of more than 0.5 suggest strong interaction and the need for either a separate scorecard or a matrix of attributes in the single scorecard.

As was mentioned in chapter 8, CHAID or neural networks can be used to identify interactions between attributes.

Credit cards vs Source

Odds			
	%	**Affinity**	**Other**
No	*19%*	0.85	0.26
Yes	*81%*	1.53	0.88
%	*100%*	68%	32%

Figure 14.4 Example Interaction Index calculation matrix

Portfolio analysis

The scorecard is only one possible cause of an increase in delinquency. The starting point is to apply tests to the key portfolio metrics to identify whether the Observed performance significantly differs from the Expected. If, for example the delinquency after 6 months is 2.1% and the Expected outcome is 1.8%, the analyst should test the hypothesis that the 2.1% outcome is possible with some degree of confidence. The test will either be the z-test for Normal distributions or the t-test where there are small numbers of readings (less than 30). Both of these tests and the confidence tables are detailed in Appendices iii and iv.

The principle should always be to drill down into the data, identifying a significant variation and then analysing it further for the cause.

Other data analysis tests include the Relative Risk Ratio, the Odds Ratio and Chi-Squared. The Relative Risk Ratio is a test to establish whether two Bad rates are significantly different. It is used when looking the strength of the association between the presence of a factor and the occurrence of an event.

$$\text{RRR} = \text{Bad rate (x) / Bad rate (y)}$$

For example if we are comparing two override codes and Code A has a Bad rate (x) of 5.6% and Code B has a Bad rate (y) of 4.8%, the Relative Risk Ratio is 5.6%/4.8% = 1.16. Therefore there is a 16% difference between the two. The significance of this could be found by finding the error using either the z-test or t-test.

The Odds Ratio is a similar test and provides a non-graphical alternative to score-odds analysis or a general comparison.

$$\text{Odds Ratio} = \text{Information Odds (x) / Information Odds (y)}$$

Where x and y are attributes. Care should be taken when applying these ratios because the scorecard itself may be the cause of variations. Since applications are rejected, the performance of accepted accounts overall will not reflect the performance of all accounts had they been approved and performance will vary by score. For example, it would not be a fair comparison to analyse the risk associated with underwriter overrides and compare this with all non-overriden Accepts.

Score-odds
Figure 14.5 shows the bad rates for the grouped attributes of Time at address. It would appear that the applicants stating they have

been exactly 3 years at their address are the problem, with almost twice the average risk. However further analysis is required to pin point the issue. It could be that this is the expected performance for '3 years'.

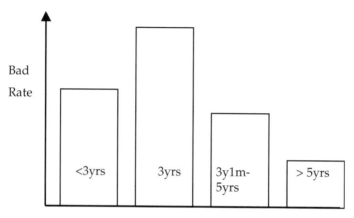

Figure 14.5 Characteristic Analysis example: Time at Address

To know whether the scorecard is the problem, we need to look at the performance by score for each attribute. This characteristic sore-odds analysis is often shown graphically. Figure 14.6 demonstrates the misalignment of the attribute '> 5 years'. This is the simplest problem and it is resolved by adjusting the point scores of the problem attribute to bring the score-odds curve in line with expectations. If the issue does appear to be '3 years' the analyst should be prepared to look for non-scoring causes.

In this example, the worse performance was caused by an operational default. The policy was that if the time at address was less than 3 years, then a previous address was required and bureau searched. If the applicant left Time at address blank, the operators entered '3 years' so that the application could be processed.

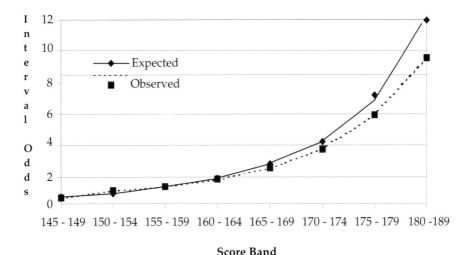

Score Band

Figure 14.6 Score-odds example for > 5 years at address

Conclusion

If the overall Bad rate varies significantly from expectations this does not mean that the scorecard has broken down. The important factor is that the principle of ranking the risk still applies or that the interval odds are as predicted.

Analysis should be as if peeling the layers of an onion: identify an issue and drill deeper to find the cause. This approach not only removes unnecessary work and mounds of paper it focuses on the problem. If a new scorecard is required, the analyst will have gained an insight into the workings and sensitivities of the scorecard and will. As a result, subsequently build a more robust scorecard.

In performing the analysis there are three main questions the analyst should be addressing as he/she digs deeper:
- Is there a problem characteristic?
- Is this a different population?
- Is there a sub-population?

The appropriate solution will depend on the answers. A problem characteristic or characteristics can be corrected by fine-tuning i.e. adjusting the point scores from the associated attributes. A different population will require a new scorecard. A sub-population may either require its own scorecard or receive special treatment within the existing one.

The process starts with the Stability Index and Average Score tests. Remember that these tests only work for characteristics included in the scorecard and the Chi-Squared test is appropriate for analysing other potential variables. The characteristic odds analysis shows the comparative performance of attributes. This is commonly checked by eye, looking for inconsistencies: typically the acceptance rate should be higher where the bad rate is lower. There are no standard tests for significance although contingency tables and the ratio of observed and expected information odds are often used. The latter can provide a score shift analysis. In other words, given the difference in outcome, how much should the point score be shifted to compensate.

There is not one magic formula for identifying whether the scorecard is a problem. Rigorous problem solving techniques are as important and scorecard analyses and whilst 'jumping to conclusions' should be avoided, there is no substitute for experience.

15

The Marketing and Dealer Effect

Incentives

In the mid 1980's in the UK, store cards were seen as the source of developing a marketing database, with analysis providing insights into the purchasing patterns and attributes that could influence the merchandising and buying. One department store (let's call them Leeder), along with many others, decided that the best way to build a massive customer base was to provide incentives to take out a store card.

Characteristics	Standard	Promotion
Owners	67.8%	80.8%
Time at Address > 5 years	39.3%	40.4%
Time in job < 3 years	58.7%	55.1%
Age > 40	32.7%	31.4%
1+ credit cards	66.3%	80.3%
Adverse credit bureau	5.1%	2.7%

Table 15.1 Key characteristics of the store card customers

Leeder introduced an incentive of 10% off for the first week after opening an account. The promotion ran for three weeks. Every quarter the promotion was repeated and continues to run in a similar form today. Table 15.1 illustrates the shift in profile from no promotion to a 10% initial discount.

The customer profile for the Leeder cards improved during the promotions. The most dramatic increases were of owners and applicants with an existing credit card. The profile of applicants improved and along with that, the acceptance rate increased from around 70% to more than 85%.

Performance

A tenet of credit management is 'the higher the applicant profile, the better the quality'. Figure 15.1 shows a graph of Bad rate by score for two months of new business. The dotted line is for promotion business, whilst the solid line is for business approved with no incentive. The promotion business has a higher average score and therefore, providing the distribution is otherwise the same, has better overall performance. More applicants are lower risk.

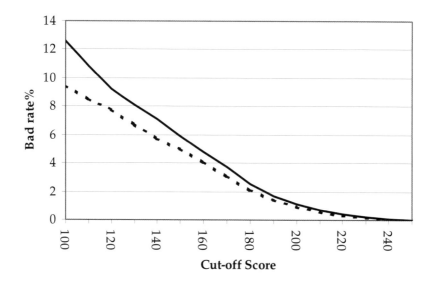

Figure 15.1 Comparison of Bad rates

This case study illustrates the principle that providing an incentive will attract a higher quality customer. A less attractive offer will only attract the credit needy, whilst a product like the Leeder store card will be used by customers who have other means to pay, but prefer to take up the offer.

Intermediaries

Many finance businesses thrive on lending to customers sourced by an intermediary. In fact, in the UK some 60 percent of mortgage applications are via brokers.

When I began my credit risk career in the early 80's, one of the rules that my experienced, credit director, boss told me was "never trust a broker". His background was a motor and asset finance organisation, which had experienced severe credit losses from business sourced by intermediaries. He also had war stories of manipulation of applications by motor dealers.

I adopted this negative view for many years and was quite surprised to discover that it was both unreasonable and unrealistic. The lesson should have been: "When underwriting an application from a third party, take care." The reality is that this is a principle that credit managers should apply to any lending situation. To set rules and systems based on paradigms is asking for trouble.

To allow quality to go unmonitored and unchecked is unacceptable today. Twenty years ago, quality was tracked at the total portfolio level and the quality of a broker's new business could be masked by an existing, larger, portfolio. Today we monitor the profile of applications, key bureau metrics and track portfolios by vintage (dynamic delinquency).

Six scenarios

To illustrate the principles of cautious credit management, let us look at some examples of business sourced using a third party. Below, are six scenarios. I will initially describe the situation for each so you can guess what the impact was on the credit quality relative to the standard or prior situation. Then I'll discuss the actual cases and impacts.

Scenario 1: The store card of a large department store had no reward scheme to boost new business. It was struggling to generate new applications so 'hostesses' were employed to recruit people in store. The agent was paid £5 per application. 'Instant Credit' was available. This meant that applications were automatically approved based on proof of name and address. Applicant's required a credit card or cheque guarantee card. The credit limit immediately granted was £200. What happened to quality compared with standard business prior to the scheme?

Scenario 2: A finance house provided unsecured personal loans for electrical goods. Loans were available up to £1,000 and approval required a telephone call to the finance house that scored and credit referenced the application. The retailer used two finance houses on a 50:50 basis. Pressure was put on the organisation to offer 'Instant Credit' and after the proposal was rejected, the other finance house launched the scheme approving 100% based on proof of address and a credit card. What happened to quality of new business the first finance house? The first finance house reacted by increasing the cut-off. At the same time the commission paid to the retailer per deal was increased. What happened to the credit quality?

Scenario 3: An Irish bank in England, used a broker to submit mortgage and loan applications to their central underwriting unit. The same scorecard and rules were used as for the main branch business. What was the broker sourced business like relative to the branch business?

Scenario 4: A non-manufacturer linked motor finance house saw acceptance rates slipping. In response, all the finance house's staff were trained in customer service. The idea was to compete on service to the motor dealers. One impact was that underwriters communicated directly with the dealer and offered to be flexible. Applications were worked to find terms that were acceptable to both the finance house and customer, rather than flat rejecting score fails. What happened to quality of the business?

Scenario 5: A bank with many years of branch lending experience used a personal loan broker for the first time. The scorecard and acceptance criteria were the same for the broker. Unusually the criteria of acceptable jobs included military personal. The bank had good experience of this group. What was the quality of the broker business compared with the standard loans?

Scenario 6: A bank provided personal loans, almost exclusively to existing customers of other bank products. When two staff left to set up their own brokerage it was seen as an opportunity to expand the business to new customers. The initial quality was dire and acceptance rates very low. The initial response to the poor quality was to give the broker notice of termination. Rather than end the relationship the new broker asked for watertight criteria. These were provided and included rules such as: on the Voters Role; has no adverse credit history; provides proof of income. There was also a strict debt to income criterion. How did the subsequent broker business perform relative to the bank's standard loans?

Over-promotion
Scenario one: We'll call the department store Wanabe. It was part of a large retail group and aspired to be Marks and Spencer. However, it was more downmarket and credit applicants were typically people who needed to make a purchase but had no other

means. A small percentage had credit cards. By introducing the 'Instant Credit' promotion using hostesses, people were encouraged to apply who, ordinarily, would not have considered applying for a Wanabe store card. This on its own could have been good news, although store cards run the risk of 'hit and runs': people who make an initial purchase, pay in full and never use the card again. This issue arises when stores promote an initial discount.

The Wanabe store card offered the applicant no benefit over and above the availability of a small line of credit. The incentive was not targeted at the customer, but at the 'hostess'. The initial profile looked very promising with a sharp increase in credit cardholders applying. The problems were realised when people complained when their new card arrived. It transpired that an alarmingly high proportion of applicants were led to believe that they were completing questionnaire rather than an application for credit.

This was unacceptable, but this in itself did not impact the performance of the book. These applicants simply did not use the facility. The problem was caused by frauds. To boost applications, the 'hostesses' cannot have seen proof of address. To support this claim it was discovered that a group of tramps had been encouraged to apply and promptly spent their £200 of free money.

Competitive pricing

Scenario two: The electrical store was Colorvision, a downmarket store. We'll call the lender Smart Bank who had many years of credit history with the store and knew the risk of lending. To compensate, the interest rate margin was higher than for comparable businesses. Estimates of the impact of unverified 'Instant Credit' were such that a policy was made that such a scheme could never be offered to Colorvision. In came as a surprise to hear that the competitor had launched 'Instant Credit'. The effect was an immediate down turn in volume of business and quality. A lower profile of applicants, equated to a lower average score which meant a higher overall risk.

An increase in the cut-off would improve the overall risk, but would exacerbate the problem of declining new business. The effect of increasing the commission was to change the positioning of the finance houses. The retailer was motivated by two things: sales and commission. In fact since more than half of all sales were on credit, combined with aggressive pricing of the goods meant that commission was a significant contributor to the bottom line.

Increasing the commission had the effect of making Smart Bank the lender of preference. In other words: first refusal. The retailer knew that the competitor would accept everything meeting their criteria and so the best business was offered to Smart. If the customer was rejected, the customer was granted credit anyway. The effect for Smart Bank was both a greater slice of the business and improved credit quality.

Unusual behaviour
Scenario three: The Irish Bank (or TIB, as we'll call them) had a long history in England and had decided to extend its services beyond the natural base of Irish ex-patriots. As well as using a broker for mortgage and loan applications, they launched a credit card. At the same time, TIB centralised back office functions including underwriting.

The performance of the non-traditional branch business was considerably worse than the branch business. The issue that organisation have in extending business is in attracting applicants they have limited prior experience of. Scorecards work best when developed on specific populations. TIB had excellent scorecards.

The problem was that they were based on the ex-patriot Irish population. These people had tremendous loyalty to their TIB branch and had characteristics that were unusual. The most extreme example was the point scores assigned for age. Unusually, younger people received more points than older – something illegal in the United States!

The rational for this is that there has been a gradual shift in the profile of Irish immigrants. Historically the Irish entering England were most likely to be labourers. Today, the young leave the Emerald Isle for qualifications and professional opportunities. Effectively the score for age reflected prospects. Clearly this logic would not apply generally.

Working the deals
Scenario four: In the late 1990's Global bank in the UK had a small branch network and a central unit which included an Hire Purchase facility to motor dealers. Relationships were typically between dealerships and the branches and were therefore non-manufacturer linked.

As manufacturer finance grew in the UK, Global bank saw volumes and acceptance rates slipping. Centralisation of underwriting was followed by the customer service program called 'the dealer is king' that was to reposition the finance house as providing a better service for dealers. In reality – although it was never overtly stated - this meant higher acceptance rates.

Over two years the proportion of new cars financed dropped from 60% to 30%. The manufacturers of the new cars also switched from the mainstream such as Ford, to a high proportion of Yugos and Ladas. In addition to 'working the deals' to increase deposits and reduce monthly instalments underwriters began to override the scorecard more.

The policy was that no more than 3% of applicants should be overrides. At its peak this was 20%. The underwriters had effectively stopped relying on the scorecards and claimed that the high percentage of score failures was due to a problem with the scorecards.

The reality was that the high percentage of score fails was due to a dramatic decline in applicant profile. This was caused by the type of customer buying the Eastern European cars and the increase in used cars relative to new. Historically only a small percentage of loans were over five years. This percentage increased sharply and since loan term was scored (longer term equalled fewer points) more applicants failed the cut-off.

The result was an accelerating deterioration in credit quality. Delinquency almost trebled in 18 months. The underwriters, instead of working with the scorecards, were undermining them with overrides and details that were changed to improve the risk. The problem with motor finance is the vehicle and deal characteristics (such as deposit, loan term, engine size, marque, deposit and so on) are often in the scorecard. Changing these details may impact the profitability of the deal, but it does not change the risk of the individual.

Comparative rules
Scenario five: The Lending Bank had a small branch network with many offices based in towns with military links. Branch managers were responsible for sourcing business and had special relationships with local large employers which invariably included the military base. Whilst loans to military personal was a small percentage overall, the performance was exceptional.

Lending to people living in a camp rather than with a stable home, required some flexibility in the underwriting. When the use of a personal loan broker was decided, no one questioned that 'military' as a job category was acceptable. Initially the profile of business via the broker appeared reasonable, however after about six months, the performance started to deteriorate. Analysis showed that it was caused by 'military'. Over 20% of applicants came from this category and performed dramatically worse than the branch experience.

The issue was that The Lending Bank was the only lender in the broker's basket of lenders who lent to military personnel. Not only were all military applicants channelled through to The Lending Bank, but the broker started to advertise to encourage applications form this group.

The Lending Bank branches typically had a relationship with the paymaster in the camp. If, in the unlikely event someone didn't pay, the money was deducted for their pay. There was no such relationship with the broker. Underwriting was not flexible, in fact military applicant's tended to provide an address, not of the camp, but of their family. This caused additional problems in chasing customer's for payment.

Targeting

Scenario six: When Direct bank's two ex-employees set-up their own brokerage, it seemed like an ideal opportunity to expand the personal loan business. The poor initial quality seemed to suggest that the trial had failed and that the bank was unable to approve broker sourced business.

Due to personal contacts at the bank, pressure was applied to try and make the business work. By setting watertight criteria such as on the Voters Role, No adverse credit, Proof of Income with Debt to Income criteria, the performance was superior to that of the existing business which was mainly driven by direct mail to Direct card customers.

The brokers changed their targeting. The initial applications had been sourced by buying lists from garages. When they were given the strict criteria, they used the electoral register and checked public records for negative information. Furthermore, when they submitted the application it was accompanied by debt and income information that could be verified.

Conclusions

Scorecards rely on the current population being like the one used for the model development. One of the main problems we face is that the population at any time depends heavily on price, promotion and the product. If any of these are changed, the scorecard may be sub-optimal. In business terms this usually means a deterioration in credit quality.

In addition, third parties can play a significant role. Intermediaries decide whose applications to pass to your business and whose to pass to a competitor. Rewarding a third party for applications rather than approvals or acquisitions can result in low profile new business. In the Wanabe store card example the scheme encouraged fraud either by the hostesses or applicants.

If there is a planned change, the credit manager should consider whether the scorecard is appropriate. Scenario three was an extreme example of this, but served to highlight how scorecards and fail to appropriately assess the risk where the population is new and unknown. If there are underwriters, can the scorecards be undermined by the underwriting? This was the situation in scenario four. Is there a conflict in the logic between the scorecard and rules? Wherever you can verify the information, such as income and employment, do so.

Change is not synonymous with declining quality. It's about understanding the competitive environment, considering who will be attracted to the offer and watching for 'adverse selection'. It is about being prepared and tracking, tracking, tracking.

16

Behavioural Scoring

Better than application scoring
Behavioural scoring is fundamentally the same process as application scoring with the exception that accounts are existing customers. This means that the performance of the account is assessed for the future treatment of the account.

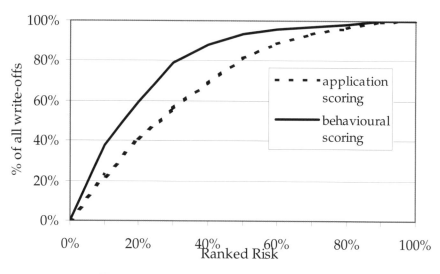

Figure 16.1 Comparison of scorecards

Figure 16.1 illustrates the power of behavioural over application scorecards. Here accounts are ranked in deciles. Effectively the ranking is the score and deciles are used here for comparative purposes. The y-axis is the cumulative write-off. The lowest scores have the highest risk and so the curve is steeper initially. As higher scores are reached, the cumulative percent flattens, reflecting the fact that few write-offs occurred for the low risk accounts. For the application scores, new applicants were approved and write-off assessed after 12 months. For the behavioural scores, existing customers were assessed at 12 months since open and write-off assessed 12 months later.

Looking at the application scorecard curve, the worst 25% of accepted accounts contribute almost 50% of the write-off. For the behavioural score, the worst 25% contribute almost 70% of the write-off. Although this is not a true like-for-like comparison because of the time difference, behavioural scoring can be seen to be significantly better at separating the Goods from the Bads.

In chapter 12 we compared scorecards using a statistical measure called the Gini coefficient. Gini ranges from 0% to 100%; from no discrimination to perfect separation of the Goods and Bads. A reasonable application scorecard may typically have a Gini of between 30% and 50%. Behavioural scorecards have a much broader range, but a scorecard for authorisations and credit limit increases, may be twice that of the application scorecard.

Development issues
Much of the power of a behavioural scorecard comes from the transaction information. This isn't surprising since this reflects the behaviour of the customer. The more transaction data, the more powerful the scorecard is likely to be. Scorecards for revolving credit products are therefore usually more powerful that for fixed term products where there is little activity other than a monthly payment.

The number of variables considered for a behavioural scorecard tends to be many times that of an application one due to the need to consider ratios since many behavioural scoring characteristics are ratios over a period, such as the average payment to instalment over the past 6 months. This means that the variables must be practical and calculable in the operational scoring system.

Figure 16.2 illustrates a behavioural scoring system. Scoring can be at cycle point, month-end or triggered by an event. The example provided is that of a cycle driven scoring system. Unlike application scoring the behavioural system relies on customer history and so the system needs to create a scoring history file. It may seem obvious that this file needs to comprise of the scorecard variables recorded over the period to be evaluated.

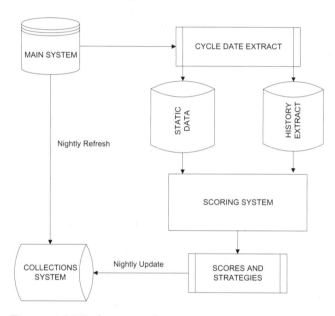

Figure 16.2 Behavioural scoring system overview

The next issue is that of influenced variables. There are two types of characteristics that are predictive: causal and influenced (or effected). The developer should consider which of the characteristics could be influenced by the business rather than be a true reflection of the cause of the performance. As we discussed in chapter 2, it is good practice to classify variables into reliable and unreliable; characteristics that should be considered and ones that should be used with extreme care. An example of an influenced characteristic is utilisation of credit limit. If the customer receives a credit limit increase their apparent risk changes. Typically risk increases with utilisation. Providing a customer with a credit limit increase will immediately reduce the utilisation and hence the predicted risk will be lower – without the customer doing a thing!

The final issue is around building a scorecard that is appropriate for the purpose. In application scorecard development we suggested that the objective of the business was critical to the success of the resultant scorecard. The same is true for behavioural scoring. Let's look at an example to see the effect of getting this wrong.

A single scorecard
The operational research team, of a mail order business we'll call Order Direct, decided to build a single behavioural scorecard for all purposes. The development was based on taking all existing accounts from the most recent month-end and going back 12 months and selecting those same accounts from that file. Accounts that were written-off or had been defaulted were classed as Bad. Accounts up-to-date or less than 1-cycle in arrears in the recent file were classed as Good.

Table 16.1 is part of the scorecard that was implemented at Order Direct. The scorecard was applied in all areas of the business: in Authorisations; for credit limit increases; for shadow limits and for early collections. With the new collections system, the scores were also passed into later collections for evaluation. Eight months after the implementation, an audit of collections discovered that the average write-off per account was approximately 60% higher than a year earlier and it was rising.

The primary cause of the increase, that the audit identified, was an issue in Authorisations. Average credit limits had doubled, this was partly due to the strategies and partly poor control over the operation. The behavioural scores were calculated monthly. Shadow limits were calculated monthly, but there was a system rule that checked for the last increase. No automated increase was permitted within a period of six months. This rule is quite common, but the operation had continued to use their discretion. In fact the rules had been relaxed so that operators were increasing limits up to the shadow limit.

Characteristic	Attribute	Point score
Current arrears	Up-to-date	50
	Past due	30
	Over 30 days	0
Number of times past due in the last 3 months	0	30
	1	5
	2+	0
Worst arrears	0	20
	1 - 2	10
	3+	0
Balance declined over past 6 months	Yes	40
	No	0
Utilisation	< 50%	20
	50% - 69%	15
	70% - 84%	12
	85% - 99%	5
	100%+	0

Table 16.1 Part of the behavioural scorecard

Aside from the problem with utilisation, there was another serious issue. Looking at table 16.1, the most powerful characteristic can be seen to be 'Current arrears'. Accounts in Collections cannot score the 50 points for this characteristic and so there is no benefit to Collections in this characteristic. Similarly, the 'Number of times past due in the past 3 months' and 'Worst arrears' are weaker for Collections customers. Accounts in Collections rarely have declining balances because they are struggling to make payments, so this characteristic is again weaker for Collections use. The 'Worst arrears' attributes '1-2' and '3+' were incorrectly assessed for collections risk. Accounts regularly in Collections were lower risk than accounts entering and potentially rolling straight to write-off.

So, Order Direct should have built at least two scorecards and taken very different samples. For the authorisations/credit limit scorecard, the sample should have been of accounts up-to-date or less than 30 days in arrears. The collections scorecard should have been developed on a sample of accounts entering into Collections. Better scorecards would have been developed if performance periods and definitions of Bad had been different.

Conclusion

Behavioural scoring is very similar to application scoring and can be considerably more powerful. However the developer must consider the practicality of variables he creates, ensuring the system can cope and is appropriate. Behavioural scoring, like application scoring must start with an agreement of the objective of the development.

Single scorecards for all purposes may seem attractive, but they will be suboptimal. It is better to be specific about the purpose of the scorecard and sample appropriately. The type and purpose of the scorecard will determine the performance period and definition of Bad.

Behavioural scoring is more about how the scores are used. A perfect scorecard is useless if it can't be implemented and the actions don't discriminate by score. However, care must still be taken in calculating variables and considering which ones are causal and which could be influenced. After all, if a scorecard's characteristics depend on the strategies then the scorecard will degrade very quickly.

17

Collections Scoring

A subset of behavioural scoring

Collections scoring is a subset of behavioural scoring, where the application is the Collections operation. As we saw in chapter 15, the predictive attributes of accounts in Collections differ from those that are up-to-date. When a single scorecard is built it is suboptimal in Collections. However, the rule of specificity applies to collections scorecards as well. A better scorecard will be developed if the developer understands the specific purpose of the scorecard and develops accordingly.

It is likely that different scorecards will be useful at various stages of Collections. For example: Early Collections, Mid Collections, Late Collections and Recoveries. The application can be as simple or broad as is required. An extreme example of a simple specific scorecard is a Citibank scorecard called 'the cheque's in the post'. The model selects customers to be mailed with the first dunning letter at day 33 to determine whether it is likely that their cheque is already in the post following the previous statement. If it is, the dunning letter is pointless and Citibank make significant cost savings by mailing only half of the customers.

Objectives for collections scorecards may therefore look at costs as well as loss through bad debt. As we'll see later they may also consider payments.

Definitions
'The cheque's in the post' scorecard illustrates the need to be specific about the sample and definitions. In this example, the sample was customers at 33 days past due (when the letter would be sent). The performance period is only three days and Bad is defined as no payment by day 36.

Figure 17.1 illustrates the different performance periods that are likely for various typical stage-based Collections scorecards. The Early Collections scorecard may have an performance period of six months and Bad defined as three or more in arrears. The sample will be accounts entering Collections. The Mid-cycle scorecard may have a performance period of two months, be accounts reaching three in arrears (or the 'Mid Collections Team') and Bads may be defined as no payment received. The Late Collections scorecard may be defined with a performance period of four months after accounts enter the area, with Bad defined as written-off.

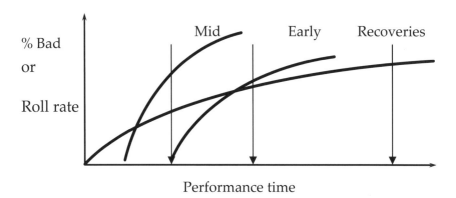

Figure 17.1 The need for different Performance periods

In chapter 5 we suggested that the Performance period be established where the 'ever Bads' flattened. In Collections it is common practice to look at roll rates over time and establish the Performance period when the roll rate exceeds a certain level. For example this could be 50% i.e. at least half of the Bads have been identified.

Recovery scores

Collections scorecards may be based on recovery information in the definition of Good and Bad. Such a score can predict how an account that is already highly delinquent will repay in the future. This type of definition is appropriate post write-off when a roll rate to a further level of arrears is less important than a steady income stream.

Alternatively the recovery information may be incorporated within the definitions in order to support a business decision. For example a business may outsource Collections or sell debt if the net recoveries from an alternative strategy are better. In this scenario Bad may be defined as recovered less than 10% of the balance.

The Dynamic effect

Behavioural scores are used to determine the risk of existing customers. We use the risk to determine the actions we want to take. These actions are to change the customers' behaviour – otherwise there would be no point in acting. However, herein lies a dilemma. If we change the behaviour the customer's score may change. This in turn may affect our future actions. This 'Dynamic effect' is an issue in Collections. Imagine an operation that calls high risk customers that are 15 days past due. Let's say a customer misses a payment but pays when he is called. Next month he misses another payment and is assessed as low risk due his past performance. He doesn't get called and as a result doesn't pay. Is he high or low risk?

The problem with scoring is that we model the past and thereby model the behaviour under the existing strategies. As strategies are changed, this behaviour can change. We are in effect trying to produce a performance that is better than predicted by the scorecard. Collections scorecards are therefore fundamentally unstable.

One approach is to maintain an environment that has consistent strategies applied to it. This overcomes the issue, but is not of practical benefit to the organization. The recommended solution is to recognise the previous and new strategies so that deviation in scorecard performance can be explained as either deterioration in the model or the impact of the strategies.

Evaluation

Due to the Dynamic effect, measures like Gini tend to less meaningful in Collections. Comparison of two scorecards applied to the same Collections scenario, is best achieved by comparing roll rates of a small number of score bands. Figure 17.2 is an example of the comparison of roll rates. Overall the roll rate is the same (it's the same population). In the example scorecard 2 has a lower roll rate for the highest score band and a higher roll rate for the high risk accounts. Scorecard 2 therefore appears to be a better scorecard.

The score bands should equate to the likely strategy splits and since we tend to have three to five strategies, there should be this number of score bands. Tracking should also be by score band, relating the actual performance with the roll rates predicted and the champion and challenger strategies compared by score.

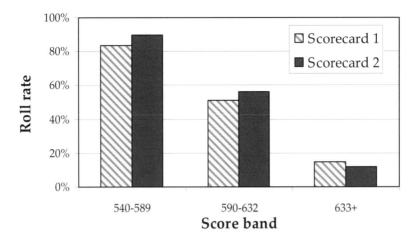

Figure 17.2 Comparison of collections scorecards

Strategy interaction

Many companies employ complex strategies that can be represented by a tree. Figure 17.3 is an example for a credit card. The collections score features in the tree, segmenting the accounts that are one payment in arrears into High (H), Medium (M) and Low (L) risk. There are other criteria in the tree: months on books, utilization and current balance.

The challenge for the developer is to understand what this tree might look like. If the business wishes to segment by balance, for example, then balance included in the scorecard will be less effective. Of course by working with the business, it could be that the developer encourages the operation to base the strategies on variables that aren't duplicated by the scorecard. In chapter 14 we considered the problem of influenced variables. Here is an opportunity to exclude them form the scorecard, but include them in the strategy tree. In figure 17.3, utilization is a good example. Utilisation drives the content of the letter rather than deter mining the risk.

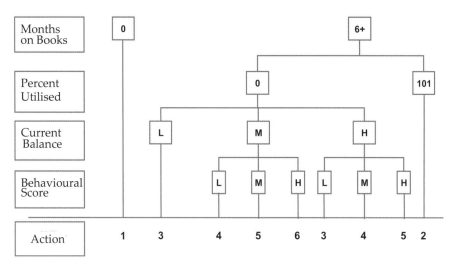

Figure 17.3 A collections strategy tree

Conclusion

The issues that apply to behavioural scorecards also apply to collections scorecards. There are many opportunities to apply scoring in Collections, but the developer must understand the business requirement and ensure that samples and definitions are appropriate to the application.

One of the biggest issues in Collections is the interaction of scorecard and strategies. This means that measure like Gini tend to be less meaningful than simple roll rate indicators for a few score bands that relate to strategies.

Bad definitions may incorporate revenue and most Recovery (post write-off) scorecards look at revenue rather than risk. However the developer should take care that his definition is not restricting the business. It may be more appropriate to have a simple bad definition and either build a separate revenue model or apply revenue rules on top of the scorecard.

The developer must take care when selecting variables that may be influenced by the strategies and should consider the segmentation that the operation may wish to employ so that duplication between scorecard and strategy tree is minimised.

18

Fraud Scoring

The fraud challenge

Fraud tends to be low on the agenda of bankers. In a 2002 survey[13] by the Centre for the Study of Financial Innovation credit risk was cited as the top concern, whereas fraud was in 18th place. However, the financial implications of fraud are considerable and credit fraud is always rising.

One can only speculate at why fraud prevention isn't higher on the agenda. One school of thought is that as part of the risk reward trade off, fraud is a small element; an operational cost to be borne by doing business. However, I believe it is a matter of perspective. Fraud detection and prevention has historically been about leg work. Most financial institutions hired ex-police investigators because they had the contacts and were diligent in their task of identifying and proving an applicant or customer to be fraudulent.

Fraud detection was just not sexy. The most successful fraud detection systems were rule based, comparing applications form the same address or person to identify discrepancies. Cases suspected as frauds but determined to be genuine are classed as 'false' whilst confirmed frauds are 'positive'. The fraud manager therefore watches the false:positive ratio carefully to determine how much manpower is used to identify genuine customers rather than fraudsters. In fact this ratio is often used to determine the success of a model applied to fraud detection.

Matching and rule-based systems

CIFAS - The UK's Fraud Prevention Service, is operated through both UK credit reference agencies and identifies the breakdown of application fraud. Table 18.1 shows the results for the first 6 months of 2005 during which over 175,000 frauds were filed with the system. CIFAS is based on filing the details at the address provided by the fraudster. When an application is received from that address, the record is flagged as a CIFAS hit, providing both the category and filing organisation to be contacted.

Category	Percentage of filings
False Identity	22.2%
Victim of Impersonation	15.6%
Application Fraud accepted	6.2%
Application Fraud rejected	44.2%
First Party Fraud	11.7%
Others	0.1%

Table 18.1. CIFAS filings by category[14]

Other available systems include Fraud Scan, CallFraud, Detect and Hunter which are rule-based and match details to previous applications. Lenders may also use in-house systems based on rules or suspect files which comprise of previous suspect frauds, suspicious names and addresses. Rule-based systems will look for inconsistencies such as a home telephone number provided as a work number on a previous application. Other rules may include:
- A weekly paid professional
- Married and living with parents

- Time on the Electoral Register is less than that on the application form
- Applicant is registered as 'off' the Electoral Register
- Multiple occupancy with similar names on the Electoral Register

Fraud scoring

Credit scoring has struggled in the fraud arena. The issue tends to be sample size. However, there is a more fundamental problem with all modelling of fraud. Modelling is about pattern recognition and fraud patterns change. Some of these changes are precipitated by the fraudsters who become more sophisticated. However, the patterns also change as companies change their approach. In the mid 1990's Barclaycard saw a significant reduction in application fraud simply due to the public launch of their new system: 'Fraud2000'.

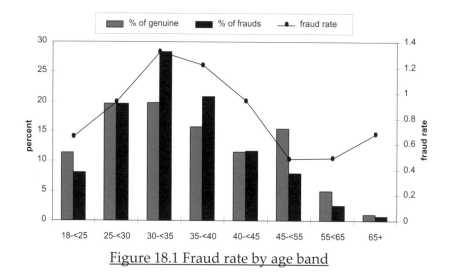

Figure 18.1 Fraud rate by age band

An example of changing patterns is mobile phone number. It wasn't long ago that mobile phone numbers had a high risk of fraud associated with them. Now most lenders would like the mobile number. On the other hand email addresses have started to show a pattern. Certain domains and shorter addresses have a higher risk of fraud[1].

Traditional scoring approaches look for linear or log-linear relationships in the data. However, a recent study by Crossley[15] of super large samples has shown that fraud rates tend to be non-linear. Whilst fraud rate increases with income, the pattern by age band showed that fraudsters were most like to give an age between 30 and 40 (see figure 18.1).

Data verification

In the ideal world all data would be verifiable so that defalcation could be easily identified. However, full verification is rarely cost justifiable and still often dependent on human interpretation. Credit bureaux have seen an opportunity to provide a service that can increase the level of confidence in the applicant's data.

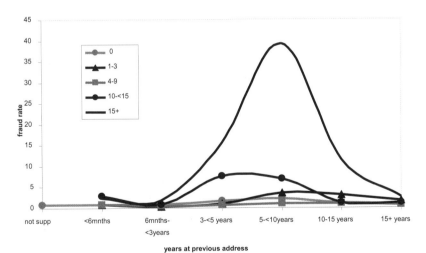

Figure 18.2 Comparing time at previous address and Electoral Roll

Figure 18.2 illustrates an example of comparing the information provided by the applicant and the credit bureau information on the time on the Electoral Roll. Each curve represents the time on the Electoral Roll. Whilst the highest fraud rate is associated with people who have been on the voters' roll, the highest relates to the applicant stating that their time at previous address was between 5 and 10 years. This is rationalised as fraudsters selecting someone from the voters' roll and guessing they have been at their address for the average UK duration. This information, combined with the growth of consortia sharing fraud data has enabled fraud scoring to shake off it's historical issues of poor false:positive ratios and become more widely employed.

Neural networks

We discussed neural nets in chapter 8. Neural networks are used extensively to identify transaction fraud on credit cards, the leading product being Falcon. In this environment, neural networks out perform scorecards due to the high volume of data and complex patterns. Neural networks benefit from being able to identify interactions in the data that a developer would need to build multiple scorecards to represent.

Typical fraud characteristics relate to out-of-pattern transactions e.g. retailer code, distance of transaction from mail postcode, high value transactions, multiple mobile phone credits (large and foreign). Models look for transactions that are significantly different from 'normal' day to day transactions.

On the downside, the systems are seen as 'black boxes' and used blindly by operational functions. Since implementation and tracking is more complicated than for scorecards, it tends to be left to the vendor – always a dangerous thing. In the late 1990's I visited an operation using Falcon and reviewed the results. The 'cut-off' was set by the operator based on volumes the investigators could handle. When asked about the false:positive rate he quoted 10 to 1. I asked if he ever dipped below the cut-off and what the success rate was there. The answer was affirmative. "It's also 10 to 1, but it ranks well by balance" was the reply.

Data visualisation and clusters

Data visualisation is the graphical view of the data to try and spot anomalies. This technique is not very practical in an operational environment, but when combined with clustering can be used to develop models and rules.

Cluster analysis is the automated classification of data into groups which can be represented graphically. The fraudulent applicants tend to be outliers and can therefore be more easily identified. However the investigator must know how to interpret the results if the system is to be useful and so practical applications in volume environments is limited.

Conclusion

Historically, rule-based systems have been favoured over fraud scoring solutions for application fraud detection. The reason has been due to low numbers of frauds to model and the issue that application fraud patterns change.

New technologies are widely used in transaction fraud detection and achieve operationally acceptable false:positive ratios. However, the rigor that we apply to tracking scorecards must also be applied to tracking and managing the 'black boxes'. It is too easy for the scoring experts in the business to abdicate responsibility for the new technologies because they are typically owned by the operational functions.

Fraud identification using the standard scoring approaches is proving itself as data pools are established and grow. The incorporation of bureau data to verify application information is also providing more robust characteristics that identify manipulated data rather than merely a profile of a fraudster. However, scoring should not be used in isolation. Combined with rules-based and application matching systems fraud scoring can be an important element in an arsenal of prevention tools.

19

Customer Scoring

Customer rather than account

If an existing customer applies for an additional loan or facility, shouldn't they be assessed based upon their existing performance? The more we know about an applicant the better our decision and so it usually (although not always, I've found) makes sense to treat existing or former customers differently. These applicants usually justify a separate scorecard; one which takes account of the performance of their existing or previous products.

Of course there are requirements for this customer approach. The portfolio must have enough cross-holdings or returning customers to justify the modelling and linking of data. In addition, the application system must have:

- Customer identification, to match applicants to existing accounts;
- Data available, to provide characteristics based on performance of those accounts.

Behavioural scoring

If a customer has a range of credit products, it would be prudent to consider a holistic view of the customer rather than to consider the performance of a single account. Imagine a customer has a credit card that has been used well and qualifies for a credit limit increase. However the customer also has a personal loan that is in arrears. Would you give the customer a limit increase on the credit card? I suspect not. The simplest customer centric system is to consider rules overlaid on top of the account based behavioural score. In this case the rule could be that the account qualifies for an increase provided that the other accounts are up-to-date.

A more advanced approach is to develop a customer score; a single score that incorporates all the products of the customer. However, this raises a lot of questions for the developer. What should the definition of Bad be by product? Should all the performance periods be the same? What about customers who don't hold all products?

This last question is crucial. If a scorecard is built on one portfolio to lend an additional product, the sample should be the customers who take up the second product. Otherwise, the performance will not be as predicted. One issue is self selection. Another is adverse selection, where the higher risk customers take-up an offer and therefore perform worse than anticipated. So if we have a range of products, the developer should ask what the customer score is intended to do. If it is to cross-sell additional products, then the scorecard will require a sample of those taking the additional product.

Revolving products may become dormant. However, they may be reactivated and high losses can be incurred by 'sleepers' – customers who start using the credit only when they are maxed out on their other products. The modeller must therefore decide whether to include dormant accounts and if so how to incorporate their risk.

The next issue is the time of scoring. If the systems are not integrated there may a problem combining the data. The modelling environment might have all the data, but is it representative of the operational environment? Imaging a mortgage portfolio that cycles at month end. There is also a credit card portfolio that is scored at individual cycle dates and a personal loan portfolio that cycles on the last day of each month. The effect will be that the data captured will be at various times during the month.

Combining risks

In the late 1990s a major UK bank developed customer level scores for use in Collections. The implementation coincided with a new customer centric system. The concept was that any collector could work any account and since a high proportion of customers had multiple accounts one call could resolve a number of collections issues. In addition the collections score would depend on all products and so enable a better assessment of the customer's willingness and ability to pay.

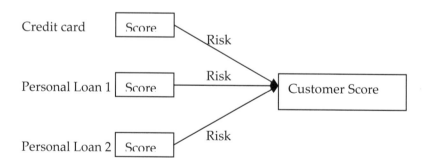

Figure 19.1 Combining scores to form a customer level score

Within a matter of months the customer level was removed. What had happened is that mortgage accounts were being collected on whereas the credit card portfolio deteriorated rapidly. The problem was explained as one of prioritisation. The high balances on the mortgages dominated both the prioritisation and the productivity. The group risk manager said "It was a wake up call to the Collections risk team. The theory was great, but practically the initial solution didn't work."

The solution to the problem, followed by many companies is to develop separate models and combine them to provide a customer score. Figure 19.1 illustrates how this is achieved. To achieve this, the scorecards must be aligned. The weights applied to each scorecard must also be determined.

The alternative solution is to convert the scores into risk and use balance at risk, since this is a pseudo measure for profitability. Figure 19.2 illustrates the combinations of risks. One issue is that the business must decide what weight should be applied to each risk. In other words, the risk associated with a credit card may be higher than that of a personal loan or overdraft. To reflect this companies weight the contribution of each risk estimate in the overall calculation of risk.

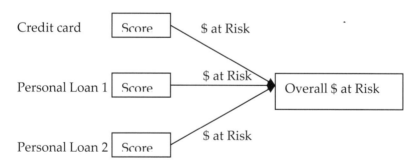

Figure 19.2 Combining risks to form a customer level risk

Domination
Customers use one financial vehicle to pay another. If the business has the cheque account and other products, it will often find that the performance of the other products is less significant than that

of the cheque account. Imagine the payments for the personal loan and credit card accounts are made from the cheque account. The cheque account has an overdraft facility and it is allowed to go over limit occasionally. The loan and credit card will not be in arrears unless the customer exceeds the overdraft.

It needn't be an overdraft facility that is dominant. In the mid 1980's HFC Bank found that the revolving loan facility was being used by many customers to pay loans and cross-fired cheques kept accounts up-to-date until credit limits were reached.

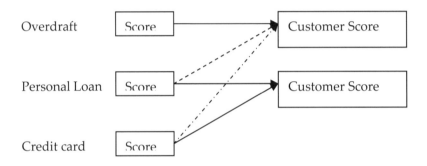

Figure 19.3 Combining scores where products dominate

Figure 19.3 illustrates a solution to customer scoring where a product dominates. The dotted lines reflect 'no risk' inputs. Transaction information may influence the score, but the payment information is not predictive. However, there will be customers who do not have an overdraft or do not pay the other products. These customers will have a customer score that is dependent on the payment performance of the accounts. This second scenario is therefore a separate customer score.

Conclusions

Customer level scoring is less about score and more about the strategy that is based on the financial value or risk. The developer should focus on the business need prior to development and ensure (as with any scorecard) that the requirements are understood and the sample is appropriate to the decisions to be made.

Particular attention must be paid to dominant accounts and dormant products. Mortgages may require special treatment or be excluded from the calculation due to the secured nature and instalment size relative to higher risk products. Companies combine risks by weighting products differently to reflect the likelihood of loss that is not otherwise reflected by the Bad definition. The severity of the loss must also be considered and companies address this by looking at the balance at risk rather than simply the bad rate.

Customer scoring can deliver significant business benefits throughout the operation. The benefits can be cost saving, such as through single-contact collections or through exposure control by considering the balance outstanding on all the customer's products. However the scores must be created with care and a single customer level score is unlikely to be as good as a model based on combining risks.

Customer scoring should be a means to an end and not the converse. Solutions must be practical and implementable.

20

Bureau Scores

The bureau score

Generic credit bureau scores were first used in the US in 1987 and quickly gained wide acceptance. The first bureau score was developed by Fair Isaac and is called the FICO score. In the US, FICO score is synonymous with bureau score and most of the public either know their score or know of it. Currently bureau scores are also available in the UK, Canada, Australia and South Africa.

The US has the most detailed credit bureau information in the world. Both positive and negative performance information is shared which is further enhanced by the use of a unique identifier - the social security number. Other countries have less depth to the data, more companies providing only negative data, and in the case of the UK, matching records by name and address. One of the issues is data protection. A hot subject in many countries and a pull against the push of credit data sharing. Even in the US, Congress is considering proposals to limit credit reference information, for example requiring the deletion of negative information over a number of years old. In the EC, a proposed directive would severely limit the data that could be held by the Credit Reference Agencies.

Today the contribution of the bureau score is extremely powerful. In the countries where they are available some lenders rely on them total and others use them to add an extra dimension to the decision. However, where politics are concerned, things are never static and the next decade may find data sharing - and hence bureau scores - very different.

The value of bureau scores
In the paper "The Value To Consumers Of Generic Scoring Models Based On Credit Reports" by Chandler and Johnson[16], a comparison was made between the power of US credit bureau-based scorecards. The power was measured by the K-S statistic (Spread) and normalised so that the best scorecard produced 100% discrimination and the others expressed as a percentage of this maximum for relative comparison. The best scorecard comprised of applicant demographics and full US bureau data. The second restricted the bureau data slightly to reflect the impact of a slight legislative change and achieved almost 80% of the power of the first scorecard. The third scorecard included only basic bureau data and achieved less than 70% of the maximum power.

Figure 20.1 demonstrates a comparison of US and UK scorecards. The UK scorecards are built on the same sample whereas, clearly the US sample is independent and included as a typical example. The relative efficiency has been established by setting the US scorecard to 100% as in Chandler and Johnson's paper. The scorecard using application data alone achieved an efficiency of approximately half that of the scorecard with both application data and a credit bureau score. The latter UK scorecard was 74% the efficiency of the US equivalent. The generic bureau score alone provided just over 60% of the power of the full UK application and bureau scorecard.

Even with full credit bureau data a scorecard incorporating a generic bureau score can outperform one where the credit bureau characteristics are developed on a bespoke sample. Typically, a good scorecard can be adjusted using a generic bureau score to increase accept rates by 5% with no increase in risk. This is possible because the Credit Reference Agencies build their models on a very large databases compared to the limited samples used for bespoke model development. The generic bureau score provides the additional benefit of being an independent, and relative, measure of portfolio quality. This is particularly advantageous where numerous scorecards are used by an organisation.

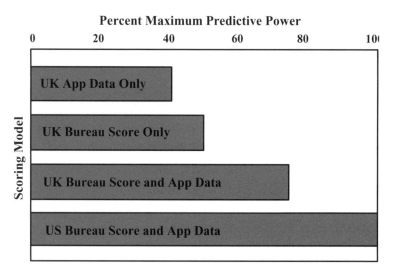

Figure 20.1: Relative Predictive Power Of Credit Bureau Detail

Application of bureau scores

In the US, pre-approval based upon the generic bureau score is common place. In 1994, for example Household International direct mailed over 80 million pre-approved offers. The techniques have been accepted to the point that the credit reference agencies develop generic models targeting specific groups.

Within application processing there are three widely used approaches to incorporating generic bureau scores within the underwriting process. These are:

Stand alone - The implementation of the generic bureau score with a cut-off without a bespoke application scorecard.

Matrix - The combining of the bespoke application scorecard with the generic bureau score providing two or more cut-offs.

Incorporation - The incorporation of the generic bureau score within the bespoke scorecard, removing existing credit bureau characteristics.

The stand alone option is the most simple and is ideal for two scenarios. Where a lender has insufficient experience to build a scorecard, a generic score provides a statistical alternative to bureau rule-based underwriting. Simple rules, turning down applicants with any adverse credit history will be significantly out performed by a generic bureau score identifying individuals who have had payment problems in the past, but are now predicted to be good.

Within any of the approaches, the Credit Risk manager should check that the system has no weaknesses. The areas to focus on are: previous addresses, address not confirmed and policy rules. Where the applicant provides a previous address, is a bureau score obtained, and if so, how is it handled? The solution to previous addresses may be to apply rules modifying the cut-off. The credit reference agency may be willing to provide guidance on this. Similarly where no match is found at the credit reference agency, a default score is likely. This should be known and appropriate address resolution policies should continue to be in place. Finally, since no scorecard is perfect, the business may wish to set criteria for policy declining very serious adverse references.

For example, the applicant may be rejected, irrespective of score, where the total of written-off accounts is higher than say £2,000.

Let's now look at the two options for combining scores.

The matrix

Figure 20.1 demonstrated the power of combining bureau and application data. Where the business is currently using an application scorecard two options should be considered. Combining the application score with the bureau score in the form of a matrix is the most straightforward. Figure 19.2 shows how cut-off strategies can be set by cells: the previous application scorecard cut-off is modified by bureau score. Lower bureau scoring applications may require a higher application score to be accepted whilst higher bureau scoring applications will be more likely to be accepted.

App Score	Missing	<500	500-599	600-699	700-799	800+	Total Bad Rate
				Bureau Score			
<95	24.6%	10.7%	10.2%	22.6%	24.8%	30.6%	23.3%
95-104	15.6%	8.7%	11.1%	9.8%	13.3%	14.2%	13.4%
105-114	13.4%	7.4%	6.5%	8.6%	11.2%	15.4%	10.9%
115-124	8.3%	5.5%	6.8%	12.3%	10.2%	13.3%	8.1%
125-134	3.2%	1.6%	2.4%	5.2%	6.1%	3.8%	2.5%
135+	8.2%	3.0%	5.8%	9.9%	12.5%	19.1%	7.0%

Figure 20.2: Bureau And Application Score Matrix

A shortcoming of the matrix approach is the complexity added to the portfolio tracking and scorecard reviews. By incorporating the bureau score within the application score overcomes this by providing a single scorecard. An additional attraction of the incorporation approach is the compensation for correlation between scorecards; clearly, an application scorecard with credit reference characteristics will have a high degree of correlation with a bureau score.

Incorporating bureau scores

The incorporation approach is typically to remove the credit reference characteristics from the application scorecard and fine tune the scorecard by using the bureau score as a characteristic. The bureau score characteristic can be defined as

$$\textbf{Bureau Score Characteristic = a + b} \times \textbf{Generic Bureau Score}$$

where a is a constant and b is a coefficient removing correlation and translating the generic bureau score so that the final scorecard has the same score distribution as that prior to the incorporation. This method enables the new system to be implemented without a change in cut-off, thus minimising the impact on the business.

Bureau scores and existing customers

Credit reference agencies produce behavioural bureau scores in addition to those used for marketing (pre-screening) and application processing. These scores can be added to in-house behavioural scores in the same way discussed above. A bureau score provides an extra dimension for the strategy where the behavioural score excludes bureau information. Figure 20.3 is an example of using bureau scores for a Collections strategy.

One word of caution about using a mixture of behavioural and bureau scores: your customers are at the credit bureau and so will be included in the bureau score. It is possible for the credit reference agency to remove your customers from their calculation and in this way you can avoid double counting your own company's performance.

		Bureau score		
		Low	**Medium**	**High**
Behavioual score	**Low**	Early Default	Accelerated Action	Standard Collections
	Medium	Accelerated Action	Standard Collections	Delayed Action
	High	Standard Collections	Delayed Action	Service Call

Figure 20.3 Collection strategies by scores matrix

Conclusion

Bureau scores can be very powerful and have many applications. By their generic nature they don't provide a lender with differentiation over a competitor, but can be combined with other scores to enhance discrimination and identify groups that can be treated differently.

The matrix approach provides the business with greater flexibility and enables raw bureau data to be incorporated in the bespoke models. Provided the lender has enough data, a bespoke model should be more powerful that the generic bureau equivalent.

Bureau scores haven't been around for long in scoring terms. However, they are set to stay and will continue to propagate throughout the world. Whilst consumer privacy will undoubtedly have an impact on the data and its use, over time, bureau scores will continue to develop and mature into a broad range of services, throughout the credit cycle: from marketing to collections and fraud prevention.

21

Profit Scoring

Bad or unprofitable?

Application scorecard developers use Bad defined by likelihood of write-off rather than based on a measure of profitability. The historical reason for this was the difficulty of defining the profitability of an account. In Finance terms, profitability will be the income less the expense associated with an account over a period. Therein lies the first question: how long is the period? The truth is that the life of the account is what matters. This is not too difficult if one has a single product with a fixed loan term. Otherwise there is the complexity of varying terms and if the portfolio includes revolving accounts, the maximum term could be indefinite.

Accountants love to work on annual results. On the other hand a purist statistician may wish to have multiple models for each possible term and extrapolate profitability to eternity for customers staying beyond historical experience. The practical compromise is typically between 3 and 5 years.

The next question is: how do you allocate costs? Direct income and expenses, such as write-offs are straightforward to assign to each account, but what about the fixed and variable costs. The solution to the variable costs might be activity based costing or a similar apportionment of the customer service and collections costs. What about overheads? These could be allocated pro rata to accounts. However, the business needs to ask itself whether future decisions should be influenced by those costs. In other words, is it the marginal contribution that matters? As a guide, if writing new business will require a new office or computer hardware, then that cost should be allocated to expected volumes. If not, the costs are an overhead that, since it is not impacted by new business, should not impact the decision to accept or reject a new applicant.

Marketing is also a difficult cost to consider. Does it matter how much the account cost to acquire? The answer is yes and no. Yes, it matters in the overall calculation of the profitability of a portfolio. No, because the cost is sunk. Once a prospect becomes a customer, it may not matter what their source was and hence what the cost of conversion was. Again, it is the contribution to the profit that counts and not the historical cost. After all, why should a customer be penalised for a poor response rate? If anything, the company may want to take on more customers to compensate for an expensive marketing campaign.

A pound today is worth more than a pound tomorrow. Due to inflation, the final consideration is cash flow. The calculation of profitability will depend on the timing of the customers' repayment transactions and draw-downs. Therefore the final profitability calculation should be expressed in terms of a net present value.

So why do we use Bad? If we look at a model predicting risk and another predicting revenue, we find that the customers generating the most income are also the highest risk. The two models are diametrically opposed. In an extreme example, in a single regression-based model predicting profitability, the two cancel each other out. The resultant model is very weak.

Regression models are notorious for their inability to detect interactions between the variables. Where profitability modelling has been successful in producing good separation of the profitable versus the unprofitable accounts is by using neural networks. Figure 21.1 is a graph showing the discrimination achieved by a neural network applied to a credit card portfolio. Return on Equity (ROE) falls almost linearly throughout the portfolio, starting at over 60% for the top 10% of the portfolio, and reaching -40% for the worst segment.

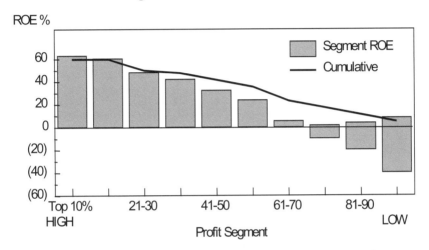

Figure 21.1 Neural net model predicting profitability

Credit risk is a driver of profitability

Risk is often confused with profitability. It is not the same. Risk is a driver, but it may not be the dominant factor, this could be attrition. If the customer leaves after 6 months, then even if they were good, the business is likely to be concerned about the profitability of that customer. If the product is an overdraft or credit limit and the customer has never borrowed money, it doesn't matter that they are Good.

Figure 21.2 shows the same neural network from figure 21.1 analysed for its prediction of delinquency. Just as the risk-based scorecard is poor at predicting profitability, the profit scorecard cannot separate the Goods from the Bads.

So in principle one can build a profit model, but that model is poor at predicting constituent parts. Since the actions taken tend to be for specific reasons, it is important that the individual drivers are also predicted. For example in Collections it is the risk or severity of loss that matters and not the likelihood of revolving.

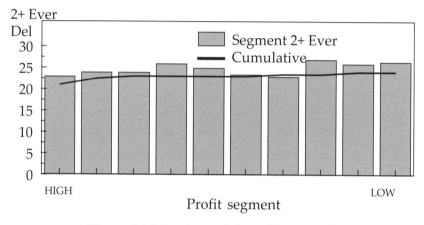

Figure 21.2 Profit model predicting risk

The driver models that should be built will depend on the product. The models (referred to as propensity models) are typically the 3 R's:
- Risk
- Reward
- Retention

A credit card portfolio may require the following propensity models:
- Attrition
- Revolve (pay interest)
- Risk
- Transact
- Cash advance

- Cross-sell (insurance, personal loan etc)

These models can be combined with one another to provide a customer value that may drive marketing strategies. Where a value is calculated, the modeller will also need to predict balances, number of transactions and should express the profit in terms of NPV. Figure 21.3 is an example of a 'customer value' architecture.

Interest Income:
   Interest Rate
     x P[Open,Active & ¬Defaulted]
     x P[Revolve¦Open,Active,¬Defaulted]
     x Outstandings:
       (Balance Component:
          0.75 x E[Balance¦Open,Active,¬Defaulted]
        + Spend Component:
          0.50 x E[Sales¦Open,Active,¬Defaulted] +
    E[Cash¦Open,Active,¬Defaulted]
        + Revolving Balance Component:
          0.25 x
    E[RevolvBal%¦Open,Active,¬Defaulted] x
      E[Bal¦Open,Active,¬Defaulted])
    - Cost of Funds

20.3 Example of a 'customer value' architecture

In the example, the interest income comprises interest from the good (¬defaulted) revolvers, based on 75% of the outstanding balance and 50% of the month's spend and 25% of the revolving balance. P is the propensity and E is the estimated value. This is not necessarily *the* answer, but for one major UK bank it provided a relative measure of profit for each customer monthly based on multiple models.

By modelling risk separately, the developer does not need to worry about who is and who is not profitable. If the business needs to know why the customer is not profitable for a reason other than bad debt, one of the other propensity models should explain it.

This logic should be applied to the scorecard development sample. In chapter 2 we said that the starting point of a development should be a clear objective. Many developers exclude dormant accounts from the scorecard development sample. If someone is dormant they may or may not be profitable. Marketing may like them because they can be reactivated. The answer is to let Risk deal with bad debt and let an activation model deal with dormant account. Risk should not try and second-guess Marketing in the risk scorecard.

The stability of profit
Profitability, like risk, is inherently unstable. The instability of risk is covered in chapter 22 on Recession Scoring. Profitability is unstable, because of risk, but also each of the other drivers has its instability. Retention depends on the competitive environment. If an attractive new competitive product is launched, a company will not be surprised that customers leave, or worse, they silently leave. The latter is an issue for credit cards where customers do not close there accounts as they would with a re-mortgage, they may transfer the balance, suddenly stop using the card, gradually stop or switch purchases to a specific item such a petrol. The competitor dramatically impacts the profitability of a customer who silently leaves and the model, based on the past, could not have predicted it.

There is another important distinction between risk and profit models. By and large the customer is responsible for his/her payments. If he/she loses income or becomes over-indebted, financial difficulty and potential write-off with result. If the bank's cost of funds changes, the customer's profitability can be impacted considerably without the influence of the customer. So there are factors that drive profitability that the customer has no control over. These factors include: operational costs, interest rates - both charged and cost of finance, marketing activity and fraud.

A US card issuer segmented its portfolio using scores to identify the most profitable. These turned out to be a group (approximately a third of the file) that was primarily made up of good customers who paid interest regularly. No surprises there! However, interest rates on competitors' products fell slightly and the card issuer was surprised to find that the profitability of this group changed over time. A high proportion of all the customers who transferred balances (40%), were from this group. Of the ones that were left, a high proportion of the write-offs (70%) came from this group, damaging the overall profitability of the group. These customers always had this propensity, but the market changed and there had been no way to forecast that the better risk customers would be attracted to a more competitive offer leaving the high risk ones to dominate the group.

Risk	Retention	Revolve	Segment
High	High	High	Reform
High	High	Low	Discourage
High	Low	High	Control
High	Low	Low	Choose to lose
Low	High	High	Golden group
Low	High	Low	Cross-sell
Low	Low	High	Re-price
Low	Low	Low	Choose to lose

Figure 21.4 Potential strategic segments

Profitability modelling has a lot of caveats. It can be useful for understanding the customer base and providing strategic direction, but as an absolute prediction of future earnings it is unreliable. As a result a feasible application is to use profit scores to rank customers for targeting the top 10% for example.

As a further step, models can be combined to identify groups for marketing activity, such as high earning potential, low risk and low activity might be a prime target for a lower interest rate offer. Figure 21.4 is a table of potential segments for alternative strategic action.

Conclusion

The 80/20 rule applies to credit portfolios, with a small proportion of customers generating most of the profit. However, profit scoring is riddled with issues. Not least of these is the problem of identifying profitability and its stability over time. The interactions in the key drivers make traditional regression models unsuitable and there has been experience of successfully using neural networks to calculate profitability. However the issue with a single outcome is its inability to represent the individual drivers of that outcome. The most important of these is credit risk, which may not be appropriately identified and segmented by an overall profit model.

The solution is to build a series of models based on the drivers and combine them to form a profit model. We looked at one advanced way this could be achieved. The issue of instability and reliability of the calculation is still unresolved by this approach. Our advice is to use the calculation if profit as a relative, rather than absolute measure. Don't worry about the exact pounds and pence, but the relative ranking. After all, strategies do not need to be precisely driven by a profitability calculation and we looked at an example of how a portfolio could be segmented based on a simple combination of models to identify actions that could be taken.

It is important that decisions are driven by profitability considerations rather than to derive those decisions from a single model. The lending business is too complicated for the latter.

22

Recession Scoring

Economic Impact

During the last Recession, many banks blamed the scorecards and indeed some turned their backs on credit scoring for a time. In a Recession, customers' incomes are squeezed by falling employment, overtime and bonuses. In the UK at the end of the 1980's, their expenditure increased as well as interest rates rocketed charging the average borrower twice what they had paid when times were good. The result is an increase in customers missing payments: bad rates and delinquency rises.

Does this mean that the scorecard was to blame? Figure 22.1 shows what typically happens. Here Bad rates have doubled in the Recession. However, the important thing to note is that the scorecard is still predictive: Higher scores have lower risk. The scorecard continues to rank the risk in a recession, but the level of risk at each score has changed.

It has to be said that not all scorecards are equal. Some scorecards will deteriorate during a Recession if the characteristics used or population is sensitive to the economy. For example, self employed customers can appear to be low risks when times are good, but during a downturn, their risk can be disproportionately high. In the 1990's Recession first time buyers were particularly sensitive to the increase in interest rates as their mortgage payment to income went from 19% to 29%[17]. Mortgages more than 6 months in arrears increased by 350% and repossessions rose 5 fold. So scorecards that targeted young owners, in particular, found their predictiveness considerably out-of-line with expectations. Other volatile scorecard characteristics are: time in employment, time at address, income and debt based measures.

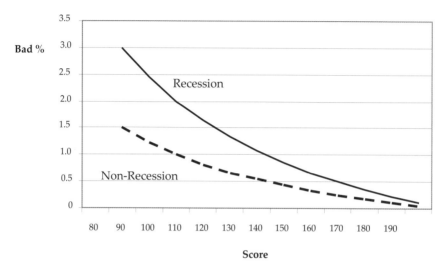

Figure 22.1 Scorecard behaviour in a Recession

As in the last Recession, one option for banks is to tighten up. However, this often happens too late and can underestimate the lifetime value of new applicants. After all the new customers will, hopefully, continue with their credit beyond the recession when risk declines once more.

The main credit management message is to identify problems early and respond appropriately. In the last UK Recession, economic indicators were lagged indicators of the impact on credit portfolios. In fact most portfolios began to deteriorate during the latter half of 1989 whereas the recession, as defined by GDP, did not officially occur until the first quarter of 1991. The key measures to track will depend on your business but are likely to include: loan to value ratios, debt to income ratios, revolving credit line value and proportion, credit line/limit utilisation, average credit score, average bureau score, first payment defaulters and roll rates.

Dynamic delinquency tables (arrears by month booked) provide a good indicator of economic downturn. In a Recession the newer accounts will typically deteriorate faster than the more mature ones. Table 22.1 shows the impact on a personal loan portfolio.

Age of accounts	Deterioration
Up to 6 months	3 x
7 to 12 months	2 x
Over 1 year	1.5 x

Table 22.1 Performance deterioration by age of account

Accounts up to 6 months old had an early bad rate 3 times higher than predicted by the scorecard, double the deterioration of the accounts over a year old. So whilst overall indicators are required, the best early warning will dissect this by time on books. For revolving credit portfolios, we recommend the Cleverness Index (Balance of a Bad divided by the balance of a Good), by age cohorts and where behavioural scoring is available, the Stability Index of average balance by score.

Score stability

Application scorecards are regularly redeveloped due to instability; how true is this for bureau scores? This question becomes increasingly important in a recession. A scorecard based on credit bureau data during a period of prosperity may discriminate well between credit-worthy and non credit-worthy customers; but during a recession the proportion of applicants with poor and detrimental bureau reference information increases sharply.

Research described by Chandler and Johnson[16] scored 5 million US individuals with the same generic bureau scorecard in January of 1989, 1990 and 1991. The scorecard predicted bankruptcy with a high score equating to a high risk of bankruptcy. The research showed that there was an upward shift in the scores overtime, with a large increase between 1990 and 1991 (the US recession), but not as large as that of the previous year. Most US lenders do not approve applicants with a bankruptcy score of 800 or more. In January 1990, 3.9% scored over 800 (up from 3% in 1989) and by January 1991 the percentage had risen to 6.1%.

So, the profile of customers, as measured by the bureau score, was falling sharply over the period and the Stability Index would suggest that there may be a problem. The critical question is how did this instability impact the predictiveness of the score? Performance was tracked with a 12 month outcome period. The conclusion was that, whilst the absolute level of risk increased, the shift in the curve between 1989 and 1990 was essentially constant indicating a constant ability to rank risk. In other words, Chandler and Johnson believed that in the US generic bureau scoring models can discriminate well whether in times of recession or prosperity. However, the instability in profile and absolute value of risk means that the Credit Risk Manager should track score distributions and performance and be ready to modify strategies as required. One lesson that we have learned over the past three economic cycles is that it is never the same twice.

Cyclicality in scorecards

Due to the accuracy of the prediction required for Capital Adequacy purposes (see chapter 23), some developers have incorporated economic indicators into the scorecard. The idea is that as the economy varies through the cycle, the predicted risk will vary. The challenge with this is the history required to build the model. Ideally data is required throughout a cycle. A further downside is that experience of the past Recessions has been variable. Most recent Recessions have differed greatly from the 1990's UK Recession. The 1998 Asian Recession impacted white-collar workers as investments were impacted more than incomes. The Recessions throughout Europe since the turn of the century have coincided with historically low interest rates and had minimal impact on scorecard predictions.

An alternative approach is to build a conversion model that takes the bad rate from the scorecard and predicts the performance, based on current economic indicators. The article by Fernández[18], discusses a solution for Banco Pastor in Spain where macroeconomic variables: GDP, unemployment and inflation are used to convert the output into a predicted performance. There is no discussion of how this was achieved. It is still likely that assumptions will be required in interpreting the conversion of the economic indicators into customer performance. However, what this approach does provide is the ability to set parameters and compare the outturn with expectations, thus enabling the factors to be tuned.

Conclusion
The business we are in suffers from cycles. Delinquency rises and falls with the affordability of the population although performance tends to lead the typical indicators of a Recession. Scorecard predicted bad rates wax and wane with the overall performance although evidence suggests that even credit bureau scores continue to rank risk. The stability of the scorecard will depend on the mix of characteristics. If there are unstable characteristics or groups that are targeted, a scorecard may be unreliable during a Recession, although this is the exception rather than the rule.

In the past some lenders have rejected scoring due to the change in predictiveness in a Recession. It is possible to build scorecards incorporating economic indicators. The alternative approach is to adjust the credit policies and cut-offs in line with the changes in risk.

Our advice is to understand where in the cycle your model data comes from and bear this in mind when tracking. During the development identify characteristics that may be sensitive to changes in income and expenditure, especially interest rates. These characteristics should be avoided if possible. It is better to adjust cut-offs or tune a scorecard during a downturn rather than redevelop the scorecard. After all, with an average Recession of 12-14 months, it will be too late by the time there is enough history for the model sample to develop and implement a new scorecard.

Whichever approach you consider, do consider an approach. Changes are occurring constantly. The degree to which a change will impact a scorecard will vary. However, one thing should remain constant; Credit Managers must keep an eye on the marketplace, the economy and the regulations. Scorecards should not be rejected because their predictiveness wakes and wanes. Scorecards should be accepted with their limitations and those limitations should be understood.

23

Capital Adequacy Scoring

IRB Approach

The Basel II Framework permits retail banks to calculate their own capital requirement based on a series of models: Probability of Default (PD), Exposure at Default (EAD) and Loss Given Default (LGD). The one we will consider here is the PD model since it is typically a scorecard not dissimilar from those we have discussed so far in this book and about which the issues and techniques apply. For simplicity in this chapter, I will assume that Default equates to 'bad'. In reality the modeller will need to evaluate the bad definition used for the scorecard development to ensure it meets the Regulators' required definition of Default.

There are issues that the calculations need to address, such as the relationship between Gini (scorecard discrimination) and capital adequacy and the regulations will evolve over time. However, there are some important principles that the PD model must follow that will be consistent over time.

The first is that it is not the model that needs to comply with regulations, but the prediction. This means that any approach may be used, provided the outcome can be justified to the Regulator. The second issue is accuracy of the prediction. Historically in credit scoring, we have been less concerned with the bad rate and more concerned with the alignment of the scorecard. If the bad rate deteriorates for a score band, but analysis shows that the scorecard continues to rank bad rate by score, a redevelopment is not recommended. For capital adequacy purposes, we not only need to understand the accuracy of the prediction, we should also consider whether there is a real difference between predicted bad rates.

Error

All models are based on samples and sampling means statistical error. How often do we ask a developer to provide information about the error on the bad rate prediction? In the past, the answer was 'never'. For Capital Adequacy purposes, the answer should be 'every time'.

Figure 23.1 shows the output of a scorecard developed on a sample of 7063 Goods and 308 Bads.

Scoreband	Total	Goods	Bads	Bad rate
-330	146	44	102	69.9%
-340	82	33	49	59.8%
-350	85	26	59	69.4%
-360	77	32	45	58.4%
-370	66	39	27	40.9%
-380	77	49	28	36.4%
-390	91	66	25	27.5%
-400	125	105	20	16.0%
-410	150	127	23	15.3%
-420	189	162	27	14.3%
-430	269	241	28	10.4%
-440	345	332	13	3.8%
-450	353	347	6	1.7%
-460	361	344	17	4.7%
-470	410	402	8	2.0%
-480	502	494	8	1.6%
-490	663	658	5	0.8%
-500	928	920	8	0.9%
-510	316	315	1	0.3%
-520	195	194	1	0.5%
>520	70	70	0	0.0%
Total	5500	5000	500	9.1%

Figure 23.1 Bad rates by score

If we assume a normal distribution of errors around each predicted bad rate, we can estimate the standard error based on the sample size. The estimate is calculated for each score band using:

Standard error = (Bad rate x Good rate)/ Total)^0.5

95% of the time the Bad rate will be less than Bad rate + 1.96 x the standard error. This figure is the Upper Confidence Limit (UCL) at the 95% confidence level. Figure 23.2 shows the standard error and UCL for the scorecard.

Scoreband	Bad rate	Standard error	UCL
-330	69.9%	3.8%	77.3%
-340	59.8%	5.4%	70.4%
-350	69.4%	5.0%	79.2%
-360	58.4%	5.6%	69.4%
-370	40.9%	6.1%	52.8%
-380	36.4%	5.5%	47.1%
-390	27.5%	4.7%	36.6%
-400	16.0%	3.3%	22.4%
-410	15.3%	2.9%	21.1%
-420	14.3%	2.5%	19.3%
-430	10.4%	1.9%	14.1%
-440	3.8%	1.0%	5.8%
-450	1.7%	0.7%	3.0%
-460	4.7%	1.1%	6.9%
-470	2.0%	0.7%	3.3%
-480	1.6%	0.6%	2.7%
-490	0.8%	0.3%	1.4%
-500	0.9%	0.3%	1.5%
-510	0.3%	0.3%	0.9%
-520	0.5%	0.5%	1.5%
>520	0.0%	0.0%	0.0%

Figure 23.2 The confidence limits of the bad rates

In chapter 6 we looked at sample size. Here we can see that the size of the sample has a considerable impact on the accuracy of the prediction. However, it is not the number of Bads that matters, but rather the number in the score band. Reducing the number of score bands will increase sample size and hence accuracy within a score band. We will look at this next and then consider the issue of weighted samples and conversion factors.

Significant difference

The *t-test* is the most commonly used method to evaluate the differences in means between two groups. In credit scorecard modelling we can use it to identify whether there is a significant difference between the bad rates of each score band to justify separate allocation of PDs in the final model. In figure 23.1 we saw ten score bands. Let's now consider whether these are justified for capital adequacy purposes.

Figure 23.3 shows the t-test calculation comparing the row with the next row for 21 score bands.

Total Score	Total	Goods	Bads	Bad rate	df	b1-b2	v1/n1	v2/n2	t
<330	129	61	68	52.7%	201	0.1352	0.0019	0.0032	1.8840
330-339	74	45	29	39.2%	144	-0.0942	0.0032	0.0035	-1.1519
340-349	72	37	35	48.6%	143	0.1162	0.0035	0.0032	1.4242
350-359	73	46	27	37.0%	142	0.1445	0.0032	0.0025	1.9223
360-369	71	55	16	22.5%	156	0.0299	0.0025	0.0018	0.4586
370-379	87	70	17	19.5%	193	0.0565	0.0018	0.0011	1.0468
380-389	108	93	15	13.9%	266	0.0639	0.0011	0.0004	1.6275
390-399	160	148	12	7.5%	351	0.0025	0.0004	0.0003	0.0880
400-409	193	179	14	7.3%	436	0.0072	0.0003	0.0002	0.2958
410-419	245	229	16	6.5%	600	0.0177	0.0002	0.0001	0.9119
420-429	357	340	17	4.8%	831	0.0308	0.0001	0.0000	2.4227
430-439	476	468	8	1.7%	967	0.0087	0.0000	0.0000	1.2168
440-449	493	489	4	0.8%	986	-0.0121	0.0000	0.0000	-1.6109
450-459	495	485	10	2.0%	1065	0.0115	0.0000	0.0000	1.5435
460-469	572	567	5	0.9%	1274	0.0016	0.0000	0.0000	0.3267
470-479	704	699	5	0.7%	1633	0.0039	0.0000	0.0000	1.0573
480-489	931	928	3	0.3%	2233	-0.0006	0.0000	0.0000	-0.2423
490-499	1304	1299	5	0.4%	1752	0.0016	0.0000	0.0000	0.5752
500-509	450	449	1	0.2%	725	-0.0014	0.0000	0.0000	-0.3279
510-519	277	276	1	0.4%	375	0.0036	0.0000	0.0000	1.0018
>519	100	100	0	0.0%	98	-	-	-	-

Figure 23.3 Testing the difference between the score bands

In the example (with a high number of degrees of freedom), at the 95% confidence level, a t-test statistic of less than 1.96 suggests that the difference between bad rates is not significant.

$$t = (b1-b2)/(v1/n1 + v2/n2)^0.5$$

where b1 is the bad rate for the score band, v1 is variance and n1 is the total number of Goods and Bads in the score band. b2, v2 and n2 relate to the next score band.

We can see from figure 23.3 that many of the predicted bad rates are not significantly different. The next process is to combine score bands until we find a series of outcomes that can be said to be different.

There is no single way to approach this. Figure 23.4 shows the result of combining the score bands until a significant difference is found and then starting with the next as a new score band. The result illustrates the impact of sample size (specifically the number of records per score band). Here we have found only five significantly different score bands for capital adequacy purposes.

Scoreband	Total	Goods	Bads	Bad rate	df	b1-b2	v1/n1	v2/n2	t
-360	390	135	255	65.4%	622	31.2%	0.00058	0.000962	7.945
-390	234	154	80	34.2%	965	20.8%	0.000962	0.000158	6.222
-420	733	635	98	13.4%	2200	10.4%	0.000158	1.98E-05	7.781
-470	1469	1425	44	3.0%	4141	2.1%	1.98E-05	3.19E-06	4.455
>470	2674	2651	23	0.9%	-	-	-	-	-
Total	5500	5000	500	9.1%					

Figure 23.4 testing the difference between the score bands

Weighted samples
Computing power today doesn't require sampling, but many developers still like to reduce the original sample, sometimes into equal numbers of Goods and Bads. In chapter 2 we looked at the *population flow* and illustrated the need for the final statistics to represent the population. This often means that the results need to be adjusted, or *weighted*, to reflect the expected outcome.

Assume that we sampled the Goods and used all the Bads. The true number of Goods was 70,030, so we need to multiply the

Goods by 14 to get bad rates that truly reflect the population. Figure 23.5 is the same as our initial output from figure 23.1 but using the weighted number of Goods to restate the bad rates.

Scoreband	Total	Goods	Bads	Bad rate	Standard error	UCL
-330	718	616	102	14.2%	0.8%	15.7%
-340	511	462	49	9.6%	0.9%	11.3%
-350	423	364	59	13.9%	1.0%	15.9%
-360	493	448	45	9.1%	0.9%	10.8%
-370	573	546	27	4.7%	0.7%	6.1%
-380	714	686	28	3.9%	0.6%	5.1%
-390	949	924	25	2.6%	0.4%	3.5%
-400	1491	1471	20	1.3%	0.3%	1.9%
-410	1802	1779	23	1.3%	0.2%	1.8%
-420	2296	2269	27	1.2%	0.2%	1.6%
-430	3403	3375	28	0.8%	0.1%	1.1%
-440	4663	4650	13	0.3%	0.1%	0.4%
-450	4866	4860	6	0.1%	0.0%	0.2%
-460	4835	4818	17	0.4%	0.1%	0.5%
-470	5638	5630	8	0.1%	0.0%	0.2%
-480	6927	6919	8	0.1%	0.0%	0.2%
-490	9221	9216	5	0.1%	0.0%	0.1%
-500	12894	12886	8	0.1%	0.0%	0.1%
-510	4413	4412	1	0.0%	0.0%	0.1%
-520	2718	2717	1	0.0%	0.0%	0.1%
>520	980	980	0	0.0%	0.0%	0.0%
Total	70530	70030	500	0.7%		

Figure 23.5 Revised bad rates by score

Revising the proportions may lead you to think that the error in the bad rate will also reduce. However, statistical error is based on sampling and the sample numbers have not changed. The figures are revised, but due to the lower bad rates rather than the number of Goods and Bads. The standard errors shown in figure 23.5 are simply found by dividing the error by the sample bad rate and multiplying it by the weighted bad rate.

Combined PD models

Aligning the management of capital and credit quality really requires scorecards and definitions to be aligned. However, on the credit quality side, we have argued that models should have appropriate performance periods and definitions of Bad that can be justified in terms of profitability. The regulators, on the other hand think in terms of annual losses and hence 12 month performance periods. The definition of Default is 90 days for retail credit and up to 180 days for mortgages.

Conversion factors may be used to convert a bad rate prediction from a credit risk model to an acceptable PD estimate. A simple example would be a behavioural score with a performance period of 24 months. The estimated PDs could be half the bad rates predicted by the behavioural scorecard. A more advanced approach to this problem would be to look at the maturity of the bad rates over time and calculate the ratio for those occurring in the first 12 months.

Where the definition of Bad does not equal the definition of default, a separate model may be applied to convert the model predictions into acceptable PD estimates. If models are combined to produce the PD estimate, the modeller will need to consider two aspects. Firstly, that the combination may take the outcome period beyond 12 months and secondly, that there will also be error associated with the estimated conversion factor.

If the model, so far considered, was for an unsecured retail credit product where bad was defined at 2 months in arrears, we will need to convert the definition to 3 months arrears (90 days). Let's assume that 50% of the accounts at 2 months in arrears roll to 3 months over a 12 month period. If this figure was based on a sample of 200 accounts at 2 months in arrears, we know that there is an error associated with this probability of 3.5% (50%x50%/200)^0.5 at the 95% confidence level.

coreband	Bad rate	Roll rate	PD Estimate	Scorecard Variance	Roll rate Variance	combined Variance	PD Std error	PD UCL
-360	11.88%	50%	5.94%	4.1%	25.0%	4.1%	0.44%	6.80%
-390	3.58%	50%	1.79%	661.7%	25.0%	661.7%	5.44%	12.45%
-420	1.09%	50%	0.54%	26.4%	25.0%	26.4%	0.54%	1.61%
-470	0.22%	50%	0.11%	28.9%	25.0%	28.9%	0.38%	0.86%
>470	0.06%	50%	0.03%	2.6%	25.0%	2.6%	0.08%	0.20%

Figure 23.6 Estimated PD combining models

Figure 23.7 shows the calculation of the PD estimate and Upper Confidence Limit at the 95% level. The standard error of the combined model is estimated by (Combined variance/(number in the score band + number on the roll rate model))^0.5.

Conclusion

Basel II has revolutionised credit scoring. Not in the sense of finding new techniques or technologies, but by integrating risk management into the profitability of the business. Historically this was only achieved via control of the bad debt, but with the advanced IRB approach to capital adequacy it is becoming a finance tool by which to manage capital.

The result has been a rethink of the design and accuracy of the risk models. Risk managers have been content with scorecards that are aligned and rank risk. Now they have to consider the accuracy of the estimated risk and therefore the error associated with that risk. The slightly different needs of the Probability of Default (PD) estimates means that the developer must consider how to convert performance periods and bad definitions into annualised estimates and PDs.

Looking at standard errors and confidence intervals will provide upper limit estimates for PD and the t-test will ensure that the business has estimates that are significantly different for each segment, or score band.

24

The Future of Credit Scoring

Changes

Comparing scorecards now with the first scorecards 50 years ago, there is very little difference. Techniques have changed very little, but improvements have been made. The significant changes have been in the growth and development of the credit reference agencies. Their data has deepened and broadened. Bureaus are springing up in most countries and moving through the stages of holding negative data, to holding both positive and negative, to developing bureau scores. The result is that the contribution of bureau data to decisions has grown and improves as the data quality and depth has increased.

Basel II has had a big impact. The primary change has been the acceptance and appreciation of scoring at senior levels within banks. We discussed the use of scores for capital adequacy in chapter 23. By requiring an alignment of risk predictions with the ability to lend and reserves, we are seeing a shift towards a more quantitative assessment of quality; a move for scoring from the back office to the CEO's office.

Credit cycle

Credit scoring has grown in acceptance and has moved from application scoring to being used at all stages of the credit cycle. The benefits of automated, objective decisioning are widely accepted and scoring has become the driver of profitability for many lenders. The side effect of the dispassionate decision system has been to bring departments together searching for the same goal: Marketing and Risk are much less likely to be seen to have as conflicting objectives; Collections operations can focus on collector performance whilst being supported on segmentation, management information and strategy performance; Fraud operations can use a broader range of tools to increase their efficiency.

Figure 24.1 Score throughout the credit cycle

Let's take a credit card example. Prospects may be modelled to identify the target market from lists. A response scorecard may be employed to ensure the profitability of responders. This may be combined with the acceptance decision to look at the profitability of conversions. At the application stage, a screening or 'Superfail' score card may be employed to identify clear rejects. This will save credit bureau costs or processing time. Where underwriters are employed, it can save their time. The application score will determine acceptance, credit limit and possibly product. A fraud score will identify high fraud risk for investigation.

At the manage stage of the cycle, behavioural scorecards take over, approving authorisations and setting shadow limits for credit limit increases or up-sell. The activity may be used for attrition models or identifying high worth/transaction customers for special treatment. Transaction fraud models may identify out-of-pattern behaviour that should be investigated.

In the final stage, a host of collections models are possible throughout the stages of collections and specific to decision requirements. At the end of the cycle there may be a litigation or agency scorecard and the Recoveries department may have a scorecard to determine their level of activity.

Wherever there is a decision to be made based on an individual's data, a scorecard can be built and employed. Bureau data and bureau scores can also be employed at each of the decision points throughout the credit cycle.

Technology

Most scorecards today are built using regression. However over the years a considerable amount of research has taken place into new technologies. The smarter we are at separating the Goods and Bads, the bigger the benefit to the business. However, as we discussed in chapter 8, for all the new approaches, it is difficult to find a consistent and real improvement using one of the more complicated approaches.

We concluded that it is more important to build a simple, understood model, than to create one that is a statistical and theoretical masterpiece that is not practical or no one understands.

One thing that has changed significantly is computing power. The affect so far on scoring has been to see the proliferation of scorecards as they have become embedded in the operating systems. However, the models are all built and implemented. Even neural networks aren't adaptive; they don't truly learn in the live environment. So one change might be a shift to adaptive decision-making models. The database against which a prospect, applicant or customer is assessed is a live one.

In a number of papers I have suggested that a bidding system could be a way forward (for example see Bailey and Hoyland[19]). This is based on the 'fly by wire' concept where planes and missiles combine multiple potential decisions to determine which is the most appropriate. Similar systems are becoming available for credit scoring.

As computational power escalates and combined technology addresses some of the practical issues of consistency and the ability to track decision quality, this solution will become a very powerful tool in the decision-making process. Figure 24.2 illustrates the principle of how the system works. An applicant is assessed on a number of 'scoring' systems and the results compared to provide a decision that may include product terms such as rate as well as the loan amount or credit limit and the accept/decline decision.

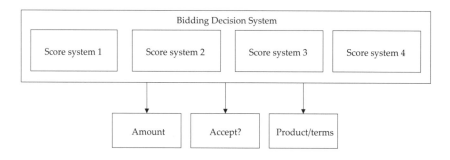

Figure 24.2 Bidding system combining models

Affordability

Affordability is core to the lending decision and yet traditional scorecards are causal models predicting an outcome after a period of time. They are simple probability models. They assume initial affordability and are said to measure stability.

The assessment of creditworthiness is not this straightforward. The reason for non-payment is more complicated than simply determining that there are good customers and ones that are bad. The traditional, human approach was to consider four elements:

- willingness to repay the debt (character);
- ability to repay the debt (affordability);
- security or collateral and;
- future prospects (stability).

The priority that the customer places on the debt (the 'payment hierarchy') varies by product. For example a mortgage is more likely to be paid than a store card debt if the customer is in financial difficulty. The size of debt also has a bearing on affordability. The credit card company underwriting based on affordability at the time of application has no idea what future debts that customer may accrue. The mortgage lender, on the other hand, has the greatest impact on current affordability and will have less concern about the future borrowing of the customer.

This means that the four elements have different roles and contributions for different products. Ability and security are the highest priority for mortgage lending and motor finance whereas understanding character and stability are essential for smaller value lending.

The mistake that some modellers make, is that they unwittingly combine all of these elements to predict a Good or Bad outcome after a period of time. The affordability and security elements are often dealt with by system or policy rules, but duplicated by characteristics in the scorecard.

The traditional scorecard modelling approach is best suited to the simple prediction of stability; if the customer can afford the credit terms today, will they be able to meet that commitment in a specified period of time? A customer who defaults immediately is either fraudulent or could not afford the credit at the outset. These attributes are clearly different from customers who get into financial difficulty at a later date and as such should be excluded from the standard model.

Perhaps the biggest change in the future will be the creation of models that are fairer to the individual. Joseph[20] suggests that the solution may lie in Systems Thinking - a contextual, as opposed analytical, approach. Instead of breaking a system down into its component parts, inter relationships are sought so that the larger framework can be understood. This may appear fanciful, but it looking to provide consumers with rights, policy makers could easily decide that assessment of an individual's right to credit should not be based on the historical performance of other customers.

Conclusion
On the surface it would appear that credit scoring has progressed little since its inception. However, models have become more predictive and are more widely employed. Modelling technology has hardly changed, but the deployment and speed and complexity of decision-making has seen the expansion of the approach throughout the credit business.

Perhaps the biggest changes have been cultural, firstly with the acceptance of credit scoring and then the regulation of their use and purpose. No one can foresee the future of credit scoring, but it would not be surprising to find that regulations move from encouraging the use of models to controlling them. With concerns regarding human rights it is easy to see that legislation may insist that credit decisions are based on the individual rather than a model. This could see a return to human underwriting, or it could be a trigger for a revolution in the way credit scoring works.

QUICK REFERENCE GUIDE

Formulae and tables

i - Kolmogorov - Smirnov Test

To test whether two cumulative continuous distributions are significantly different.

Where the samples (scorebands) are equal in number, the Test is:

$$D = t/n$$

where t is the tabulated value and n the number of samples.

Table of values (t) for critical regions 5% and 1%:

n	5	6	7	8,9	10-12	13	14,15	16,17	18,19
5%	5	5	6	6	7	7	8	8	9
1%	5	6	6	7	8	9	9	10	10

n	20-22	23	24-27	28-32	33-37	38-39	40-42	43-45	46-48
5%	9	10	10	11	12	12	13	13	14
1%	11	11	12	13	14	15	15	16	16

ii – Chi-Squared Test

To test whether a set of discrete observations fit an expected distribution the Test is:

$$X_v^2 = \Sigma \, (Obs - Exp)^2 / Exp$$

where v is the number of degrees of freedom. For the test on one distribution $v = n - 1$. For contingency tables $v = (n-1)\times(m-1)$ where n and m are the number of outcomes of the distributions.

Table of values by significance level:

2 tailed	90%	95%	98%	99%
1 tailed	95%	97.5%	99%	99.5%
$v = 1$	3.84	5.02	6.64	7.88
$v = 2$	5.99	7.38	9.21	10.60
$v = 3$	7.82	9.35	11.35	12.84
$v = 4$	9.49	11.14	13.27	14.86
$v = 5$	11.07	12.83	15.09	16.75
$v = 6$	12.59	14.45	16.81	18.55
$v = 7$	14.07	16.01	18.47	20.28
$v = 8$	15.51	17.54	20.10	21.96
$v = 9$	16.92	19.02	21.67	23.59
$v = 10$	18.31	20.48	23.21	25.19

iii - Normal, z Test

To test the hypothesis that an outcome of a test or sample arises from a population that is continuous and Normally distributed. Where σ is unknown for the population but known for the sample, z can be estimated as

$$z \cong \sqrt{n}\,(x-m)/s_i$$

where x is the outcome, m is the mean outcome, n is the sample size and s_i the standard deviation of the sample.

The Critical values of z, by confidence interval are:

Confidence	1 tailed	2 tailed
99%	2.33	2.58
95%	1.64	1.96
90%	1.28	1.64
85%	1.04	1.44
80%	0.84	1.28
75%	0.67	1.15
70%	0.52	1.04
65%	0.39	0.93
60%	0.25	0.84

iv - Student t Test

To test the hypothesis that an outcome of a small test or sample (n < 30) arises from a continuous distribution.

The test is:

$$t = \sqrt{(n-1)} \; (x-m)/s_i$$

where x is the outcome, m is the mean outcome, n is the sample size and s_i the standard deviation of the sample.

The distribution depends on the number of degrees of freedom, v.

2 tailed	90%	95%	98%	99%
1 tailed	95%	97.5%	99%	99.5%
$v = 1$	6.314	12.706	31.821	63.657
$v = 2$	2.920	4.303	6.965	9.925
$v = 3$	2.353	3.182	4.541	5.841
$v = 4$	2.132	2.776	3.747	4.604
$v = 5$	2.015	2.571	3.365	4.032
$v = 6$	1.943	2.447	3.143	3.707
$v = 7$	1.895	2.365	2.998	3.499
$v = 8$	1.860	2.306	2.896	3.355
$v = 9$	1.833	2.262	2.821	3.250
$v = 10$	1.812	2.228	2.764	3.169

v - Stability Index

To test the stability of a scored distribution.

Stability Index = Σ [(A - B) x Ln(A/B)]

where A is the observed percentage at each score band. B is the expected percentage at each score band.

The interpretation guideline for Stability Index is:

Stability Index	Stability	Interpretation
Less than 0.10	No change	OK
0.10 to 0.249	Slight shift	Caution
0.25 and above	Shift	Danger

Note: This is sometimes expressed by the multiplication by 1000 or as a percentage.

vi - Information Value

To test the predictiveness of a characteristic based on Information Odds.

$$\textbf{Information Value} = \Sigma\,[(G - B) \times Ln(G/B)]$$

where G is the proportion of Goods for an attribute and B is the proportion of Bads for the attribute.

The interpretation guideline for Information Value is:

Information Value	Interpretation
Less than 0.03	Not useful
0.03 to 0.09	Weak predictor
0.10 to 0.29	Average predictor
0.30 to 0.49	Strong predictor
0.50 and above	Very Strong predictor

vii - Conversion Equations

For the following equations: G denotes number of Goods, B denotes number of Bads, *i* denotes that the number is associated with an attribute.

Bad rate = B/(G+B)

Bad rate = 1/(Odds + 1)

Odds = G/B

Odds = 1/(Bad rate) - 1

Information Odds = G_i/B_i

Information Odds = Odds/Population Odds

Information Odds$_i$ = [1/(Bad rate$_i$) - 1] / [1/(Bad rate) - 1]

REFERENCES

1. Murray Bailey, "Building scorecards: The pits and the pendulum", Credit Risk International, Blue Moon Publishing (April 2003)

2. Hand D.J., Henley W.E., "Statistical classification methods in consumer credit", Journal of the Royal Statistical Society, Series A, 160, 523-541 (1997)

3. Boyle M., Crook J.N., Hamilton R., Thomas L.C., "Methods for credit scoring applied to slow payers in Credit scoring and Credit Control", Oxford University Press, Oxford, pp75-90 (1992)

4. Srinivasan V., Kim Y.H. "Credit granting: a comparative analysis of classification procedures", Journal of Finance 42, 665-683 (1987)

5. Yobas M.B., Crook J.N., Ross P. "Credit scoring using neural and evolutionary techniques", Working Paper 97/2, Credit Research Centre, University of Edinburgh

6. Desai V.S., Crook J.N., Overstreet G.A., "A comparison of neural networks and linear scoring models in the credit environment", European Journal of Operational Research 95, 24-37 (1996)

7. Desai V.S., Convay D.G., Crook J.N., Overstreet G.A., "Credit scoring models in the credit union environment using neural networks and genetic algorithms", IMA Journal of Mathematics applied in Business and Industry 8, 323-346 (1997)

8. Oxley J. internal research by Experian, results reported in "Not all scorecards are the same", Credit Risk International, Blue Moon Publishing (May 2003)

9. Hand D.J., Henley W.E., "Can reject inference ever work?" IMA Journal of Mathematics Applied in Business and Industry, 5, 45–55. R54 (1993/4)

10. Poole D., "A Users Perspective", Credit Scoring Principles and Practicalities 2nd edition, White Box Publishing (2004)

11. Burns P. and Ody C. "Forum on Validation of Consumer Credit Risk Models", The Wharton Financial Institutions Centre (Nov 2004)

12. Annis C. See www.statisticalengineering.com/r-squared.htm

13. Lascelles D. "Banana Skins 2002", Centre for the Study of Financial Innovation, London UK, February 2002.

14. CIFAS for the latest fraud statistics, see www.cifas.org.uk/press.asp

15. Crossley, J. "Application Fraud Scoring", "Consumer Credit Quality", White Box Publishing (2004)

16 Chandler G. and Johnson R. "The Value To Consumers Of Generic Scoring Models Based On Credit Reports" Paper submitted to the IMA Journal Of Mathematics Applied In Business & Industry

17 Maclennan D. "A Competitive UK Economy: The Challenges For Housing Policy", Joseph Rowntree Foundation, York (June 1994)

18. Fernández, D. "Banco Pastor, mortgage scoring accuracy in Spain", Credit Risk International Blue Moon Publishing (June 2003)

19 Bailey M. and Hoyland C. "Recessions and Recession scoring", Credit Scoring Principles and Practicalities 2nd edition, White Box Publishing (2004)

20. Maurice Joseph "Challenging the Credit Scoring Paradigm" Credit Risk International, Blue Moon Publishing (Nov and Dec 2002)

GLOSSARY OF TERMS

Acceptance rate - The percentage of applications which are approved. See Acquisition rate.

Accepts - Applications which are accepted.

Acquisition rate - The percentage of applications which are approved and which take up the offer of credit.

Adaptability - The fit of a scorecard to a different population (see Calibration).

AI - Abbreviation for Artificial Intelligence.

Algorithm - Any computation or method involving a series of steps. The precise instructions for solving a problem.

Alignment - The adjustment of the constant and range of a scorecard to achieve a targeted risk at a specific score or value. E.g. the Odds double for every 20 points.

Application Data - The information provided by the applicant on the application form. Sometimes used to include all data at the point of application.

Application Score - Mainly, the credit score calculated on the application data alone, but also used more generally in place of credit score.

Application Processing System - A computer system or software used for processing credit applications. This may comprise the scorecard engine and strategies, workflow and rules.

Artificial Intelligence - The ability of a computer that performs operations normally associated with human intelligence.

Ascending Cumulative Statistics - A score distribution showing the percentage of applicants which can be expected to attain that score or less (see Descending Cumulative).

Attributes - A set or range of values that a characteristic can attain.

Bad Rate - The percentage of accounts which are classed as bad (see Odds and Probability of payment).

Bads - Accounts that the lender classes as those, that given hindsight, he would not have accepted.

Behavioural Scoring - A scoring system for assessing the performance of an existing account. Scores are typically risk-based but can be applied to any performance objective. Also known as Behaviour Scoring and Performance Scoring.

Bivariate Analysis - Any form of analysis in which only two variables are considered.

Calibration - The tuning of a scorecard to fit a different or shifted population. The term is most commonly used when applied to generic or bureau scores.

CAIS - "Credit Account Information Sharing" The UK proprietary loan payment history system provided by Experian.

CCJ - Abbreviation for County Court Judgement. A UK term whose equivalent elsewhere is Judgement and Decree in Scotland.

Challenger - A strategy employed as a test to be evaluated against the Champion.

Champion - A strategy employed for the majority of accounts.

Characteristic - Any variable that could appear in a scorecard. Characteristics are made up of Attributes.

Characteristic Analysis - A report on the percentage of applications (accepts/rejects/goods/bads) for each attribute of a characteristic. Monitoring reports may also include Points differences.

Chi-Squared - The statistical test of goodness of fit. Most commonly used in Credit Scoring in place of Stability Index and Information Value.

Classification Point - The point in time at which an account is observed and classified as good or bad. Also known as the Observation Point or the Sampling Point.

Coarse Classing - The grouping of attributes into larger groups for statistical significance. Also known as Grouping.

Cohort - A tranche of business, the delinquency of which is tracked over time.

Cohort Analysis - An alternative term for Dynamic Delinquency.

Concordance - A measure of scorecard power. It the percentage of times that the scorecard scores a good account higher than a bad account.

Continuous Characteristic - A characteristic whose range of possible values is numeric and infinite (or very large).

Control Group - The group of accounts against which no tests are applied when evaluating an alternative process, strategy or technique.

Correlation - The interdependence between two or more characteristics which can be explained by a linear relationship.

Credit Bureau - An organisation which collects and supplies credit-related information. Also referred to as a Credit Reference Agency.

Credit Bureau Score - A generic score provided by a Credit Reference Agency.

Credit Reference - The process of and information arising from an enquiry at a credit bureau.

Credit Scoring - The term for using a linear predictive model for assessing and ranking customers or applicants for credit. Also used more generally to include all types of predictive credit models.

Cross Counts - The tabulation of any characteristic against score-bands to show the score distributions of the attributes. Also the tabulation of any characteristic against another characteristic.

Cross Tabulations - An alternative term for Cross Counts. Often abbreviated to cross tabs.

Customer Relationship Management - The management of customers based on an holistic view of profitability rather than risk. Also termed Customer Value Management.

Customer Scoring - The general term for assessing and ranking customers at the customer rather than the account or product level.

Cut-off - The score below which applications are either automatically rejected or recommended for rejection.

Cut-off Strategy - The determination of the cut-off score.

Data Specification - Description of all the data considered when developing a scorecard.

Decision Trees - The organisation of information as a non-recursive partitioning of characteristics available, creating a connected graph with nodes branching into other nodes.

Declines - Applicants not granted the credit applied for.

Decree - The Scottish equivalent of the County Court Judgement in England.

Dependence - The overlap in the information contributed by two or more characteristics.

Descending Cumulative Statistics - A table of scores showing, for each score, the percentage of applicants that can be expected to achieve that score or higher.

Detailed Analysis - Alternative term for Fine Classing.

Development Sample - That group of accounts which is used to develop the scorecard.

Discrete Characteristic - A characteristic, such as residential status, where there is a finite number of potential variables.

Discriminant Analysis - A multivariate analysis classification technique similar to Linear Regression.

Distribution - The spread of occurrences.

Divergence - A measure of the separation of two distributions and used to measure the power of a scorecard.

Dynamic Delinquency - The delinquency of a cohort of business over time, showing percentages of arrears at each period of observation.

Exclusions - Accounts excluded from a scorecard development sample

Expert System - Computer software based on expert knowledge rather than data or statistics.

Exposure Period - The length of time an account has been on the books or the time between measurement and outcome.

Final Score - The credit score which includes application data and all other, internal or external data.

Final Score Report - A report on applications during a period, showing proportions and accept rates by score.

Fine Classing - The process of defining all the possible attributes for every characteristic, and analysing each to show their good/bad distributions. Also known as Detailed Analysis.

Forced Accepts - Applications accepted below the cut-off. More commonly called Lowside Overrides.

Forced Rejects - Applications rejected above the cut-off. More commonly called Highside Overrides.

Generated Characteristic - A characteristic created from two or more others.

Generic Scorecard - A scorecard which has been generated when there is insufficient data to build a bespoke scorecard. Sometimes referred to as a Start-up Scorecard.

Gini Coefficient - A rank order measure of the power of a scorecard and individual characteristics that is independent of score and scale.

Good/Bad Definition - The definitions of good and bad accounts used during a scorecard development.

Goods - Accounts which a credit grantor, with hindsight would lend to again.

Grey Zone - A score band between two cut-offs where the applications are referred to an underwriter for further investigation.

Grouping - The amalgamation of attributes into larger groups to reduce the total number of attributes and to ensure that the sample count for each one is statistically significant. Also known as Coarse Classing.

Hold-out Sample - Part of the development sample that is kept aside for validation.

Inactives - Credit or charge card accounts which are not active.

Indeterminates - Accounts for which Outcome classification cannot be determined. A term sometimes used in place of Intermediate.

Information Entropy - The degree to which the odds have drifted from the expected to the observed.

Information Odds - The ratio of the proportion of all Goods to the proportion of all Bads for an attribute or group. Contrast with Overall Odds.

Information Value - A measure of the power of a characteristic using Weights of Evidence.

Interaction - A statistical term for where the Bad rate of the combination of variables is not explained by the linear contribution of the variables.

Interaction Index - A measure of the degree of interaction expressed as the ratio of the Odds of pairs of attributes.

Intermediates - A specific term for the accounts which can be classified as neither Good nor Bad. Sometimes called Greys or Indeterminates.

Interval Odds - The Odds applying across a score band or score interval.

Interval Statistics - A table that shows the percentage of applicants by score.

Insight - The UK proprietary loan payment history system provided by Equifax.

Judgement - A formal decision handed down by a court of law. In respect of a debtor, an order to pay the creditor and the means by which this is to be achieved, will also be given.

Knowledge-Based Systems - A system based on expert knowledge and inference procedures.

Kolmogorov-Smirnoff (KS)- The statistical test of a scorecards separation of its Principal Sets. Also known as Spread and Maximum Separation.

Linear Regression - A linear multivariate analysis tool for identifying correlations. Also known as OLS.

Logistic Regression - A logistic form of regression analysis in which predictors are constrained to be within the range 0 to 1.

Marginal Odds - The Interval Odds at the score band just above the cut-off.

Maximum Separation - The maximum cumulative percentage difference between the Principle Sets. Alternative term for the Kolmogorov-Smirnoff statistic.

Misalignment - The situation where attributes of the scorecard are inaccurately predicting the risk.

Misalignment Index - A measure of the degree of Misalignment.

Multiple Linear Regression - See Linear Regression.

Neural Network - A system or modelling approach that is said to mimic the cells in the brain. The most commonly used are multi-layered with an input, output and hidden layer where each layer is a node or processing function.

Non-responders - Those people who do not respond to direct marketing.

Observation Period - The time between the application, or sampling point and the Observation Point.

Observation Point - The point in time at which an account is observed and classified as good or bad. Also known as the Classification Point, or the Sampling Point.

Odds - The ratio of Goods to Bads, providing a measure of risk for analysing the performance of Attributes.

Operational Grouping - Alternative term for Coarse Classing or Grouping.

Overall Odds - The product of the Population Odds and the Information Odds.

Overrides - Applications where the scorecard decision has been reversed.

Override Analysis - A report of the overrides by score bands.

Performance Scoring - Alternative term for Behavioural Scoring.

Point Scoring - Archaic term for Credit Scoring.

Points - The values assigned to each attribute of a scorecard.

Policy Rule - Any rule which is applied in addition to the scorecard.

Population - All applicants who have applied for a particular credit product.

Population Flow - A flow chart showing the breakdown of applications by performance. Often used to demonstrate sampling or performance inference.

Population Odds - A measure of the credit risk of a population. See Overall Odds.

Population Stability - A measure of the degree of similarity between the current and expected populations.

Portfolio - All accounts held by a credit grantor, typically split by product.

Pre-screening - The process of removing from a mailing list any entries which do not meet a predefined set of criteria.

Pre-screen Scorecard - A scorecard used to select prospects for mailing.

Principle Sets - The groups analysed in the scorecard, such as Good and Bad or Accept and Reject.

Profit Scoring - The statistical modelling of profit as the outcome or combination of models to comprise an aggregate profit score.

Pull List - A list of account numbers to be used in physically collecting the application data for a scorecard development.

R Squared - The statistical output of regression analysis showing the degree of correlation between score and Outcome and hence the predictiveness of a scorecard.

Raw Score - The Weight of Evidence of an Attribute. Used less commonly to mean the score prior to alignment.

Reject Inference - The process of determining the likely performance of the rejects had they been accepted.

Rejects - Applications for credit which are not approved for credit.

Responders - People who respond to marketing.

Response Rates - The percentage of responses.

Response Scoring - The ranking of mailing prospects by propensity to respond.

Roll Rate Analysis - A report showing the proportion of accounts which move from one level of arrears to another.

Run Books - the scorecard distribution statistics providing interval, ascending and cumulative figures used for setting cut-off or score band strategies.

Sample - The accounts selected to develop a scorecard. Also known as Development Sample.

Sampling Window - The time period from which the Development Sample is extracted. Also known as Sample Time Frame.

Sampling Plan - The plan for selecting representative examples of Good, Bad and rejected applications for scorecard development.

Sampling Point - Alternative term for Observation Point.

Score - The total number of points achieved by a prospect, applicant or customer on a scorecard.

Score Band - A narrow range of scores which are grouped together to form a statistically meaningful unit. Also known as Score Interval.

Scorecard - The general term for a ranking mechanism, typically using point scores, to predict an Outcome.

Scorecard Power - General term for the measures of a scorecard's strength. These may include R-squared, information value, coefficient of determination, Gini coefficient, divergence or Kolmogorov-Smirnoff statistic.

Solicitation Scoring - Alternative term for response scoring.

Spread - Alternative term for Maximum Separation.

Start-up Scorecard - A generic scorecard applied to a launch scenario.

Sub-population - Any sub-group within the main population which appears to be different from the rest of the population, either in terms of the data used for the credit decision or because a separate scorecard is required.

Super Fail - Applications which fail the first stage of a two stage scorecard.

Super Pass - Applications which are accepted at the first stage of a two stage scorecard.

Summary Counts - An analysis of the Development Sample by category and date.

Swap Set - Specifically, the previous accepts that are rejected and the previous rejects that are accepted under a new scoring system. More generally used for the cross count of all of the current system decisions against the new scoring system.

Total Odds - Alternative term for Overall Odds or Population Odds.

Tracking - The monitoring of a scorecard. Also known as Monitoring.

TTD - Abbreviation for Through-The-Door, meaning the applicant population.

Validation - The process of testing the final scorecard before delivery.

Validation Sample - Part of the development (Hold-out) sample that is kept aside for validation. May also include a more recent sample of accounts to test the robustness due to changes in the population.

Weightings - Alternative term for Points and originated from the use of Weights of Evidence to build a scorecard.

Weight of Evidence - The predictiveness of an attribute measured as the Logarithm of the Information Odds. Also known as Raw Score.

Z-score - A commercial lending score based mainly on ratios from financial accounts.

INDEX

ABOUT THE AUTHOR

Murray Bailey received a First Class Honours Degree from Southampton University in Physics and obtained a scholarship to study Astrophysics at St John's College, Cambridge where he completed Part 3 of the Mathematics Tripos. In an attempt to find something a little more practical he joined Coopers & Lybrand as a trainee chartered accountant and in 1985 joined the fledgling analysis team at Welbeck Finance. Three years later he became Credit Director at a Citibank subsidiary, Storecard Ltd before moving into the head office and covering the credit quality of all consumer credit products. In 1991 he became the Credit Director of HFC Bank and after six years, launched Windsor Consulting, providing training and consultancy to the consumer credit industry. He has worked at many of the major banks including a year with GE Capital as their Chief Risk Officer in the UK.

Murray has edited and contributed to three books: *Credit Scoring: The Principles and Practicalities; Consumer Collections and Recoveries: Operations and Strategies, and; Consumer Credit Quality: Underwriting, Scoring, Fraud Prevention and Collections.* He has written a light hearted book statistics called *Lies, Damn Lies and Statistics in Consumer Credit.* He spent a year editing the magazine *Credit Risk International* and has also been published in *Credit Today* and *iSixSigma Financial Services.*